# The Kingdom of the Kid

Also by Geoff Gehman

*Down But Not Quite Out in Hollow-weird:*
*A Documentary in Letters of Eric Knight*

# The Kingdom of the Kid

## of the Kid

### Growing Up in the Long-Lost Hamptons

#### Geoff Gehman

excelsior editions

State University of New York Press
Albany, New York

Cover: The author, then 10, and his sister Meg, 6, on the author's favorite beach by Beach Lane in Wainscott, Long Island, September 1968.
*(Gehman Family Collection)*

Published by State University of New York Press, Albany

© 2013 Geoff Gehman

Excelsior Editions is an imprint of State University of New York Press

For information, contact State University of New York Press, Albany, NY
www.sunypress.edu

Production by Diane Ganeles
Marketing by Kate McDonnell

**Library of Congress Cataloging-in-Publication Data**

Gehman, Geoff.
  The kingdom of the kid : growing up in the long-lost Hamptons / Geoff Gehman.
        pages cm. — (Excelsior editions)
  Includes bibliographical references.
  ISBN 978-1-4384-4784-1
  1. Gehman, Geoff—Childhood and youth.  2. Hamptons (N.Y.)—Biography.
3. Boys—New York (State)—Hamptons—Biography.  4. Hamptons
(N.Y.)—Social life and customs—20th century.  5. Middle class
families—New York (State)—Hamptons—History—20th century. I.  Title.

  F127.S9G44 2013
  974.7'21—dc23                                              2012045680

10 9 8 7 6 5 4 3 2 1

*For Dad,*
*who settled and unsettled us*
*on the South Fork*

The author's father, Clarence Harvey "Larry" Gehman, already a snake charmer at age 2. *(Gehman Family Collection)*

All my changes were there.

—Neil Young, "Helpless"

# CONTENTS

The Hamptons portion of an old map of Long Island that hung in the author's childhood bedroom in Wainscott; for some reason artist Court-

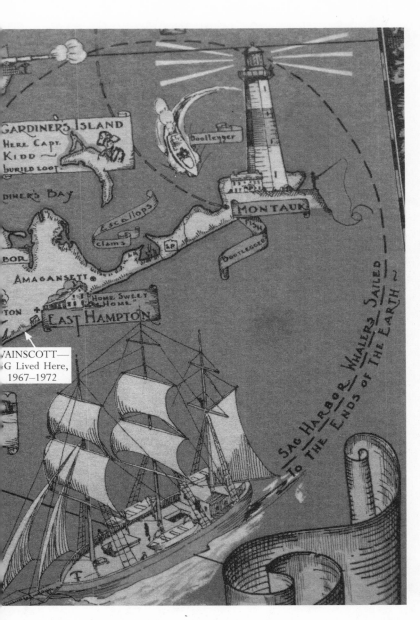

land Smith failed to include Wainscott. *(Photo by Theo Anderson. Map published by The Billboard Barn, Southampton, L.I. Copyright 1933, 1961)*

# Special Deliveries

Lobsters lined up for a race on the Kaufman porch, winner to be dunked first in a pot of boiling water, August 1967. Lobster handlers are, from left, the author, Whitley Kaufman, Meg Gehman, Clayton Kaufman. *(Photo courtesy of Clay Kaufman)*

In the summer of 1969 astronauts opened the moon, Woodstock rockers closed the New York State Thruway, and I began delivering the U.S. mail with Yaz.

The route, and routine, was virtually the same virtually every morning in Wainscott, N.Y, a hamlet of 500-odd folks on Long Island's South Fork, the farm community and beach resort also known as the East End and commonly called the Hamptons. First I hopped on my Stingray bicycle, the one with the banana seat and the spokes clipped with eight years of baseball cards starring Carl Yastrzemski—Bridgehampton native, Boston Red Sox hero and my first role model who wasn't my parents. Then I crossed Whitney Lane to the Graves' newspaper box to borrow their *Newsday* to check Yaz's latest box score. After returning the paper to its proper place, I cycled to the main drag, Sayre's Path, a slightly humped, lightly sandy lane splitting woods of scrub oak and fields of potatoes. Pumping furiously, I passed the screened porch where Paul McCartney played guitar during his early months as an ex-Beatle and the yard where a well-off, well-oiled Scottish chauffeur named Pete Morrison toasted the sunset by playing "Amazing Grace" on bagpipes.

At the end of the path I stopped to soak in the fabulously wet, amazingly graceful South Fork light, which bounces off the Atlantic Ocean and a half-dozen other kinds of waterway, turning the sky into a sea of silky scrim and everything else into crisply outlined islands. Turning right onto Main Street, the rare main street in America without a single working store, I pedaled by maples and lindens planted after the 1938 hurricane, three centuries' worth of six architectural styles, a potato-dairy-strawberry farm owned by a family who came here from southern England in the northern half of the seventeenth century, and a nineteenth-century church that began life as a Bridgehampton school. Beyond the chapel was a holy quartet of earthy landmarks: a rectangular cemetery where I learned to meditate on mortality; a rectangular baseball field where I hit foul balls off gravestones as a member of the Wainscott Wildcats; a one-room school house where my wildcat sister contemplated her misbehavior in a trash can, and a dead general store I resurrected with my imagination.

Near the western end of Main Street I parked by a shingled cottage that served as a one-room post office. After removing the mail from our box, I saluted postmistress Ethel Pierson, a former New York City teacher with a remarkable collection of seashells and life preservers and a husband who was a carpenter comic. (Asked why the post-office flag flew at half-mast, Sam Pierson quipped: "For the death of the three-cent stamp.") Before leaving the premises I scanned the FBI's most-wanted list, memorizing the frightening faces of violent criminals just in case I met them roaming Beach Lane beach, disguised in sunglasses, bathing suits and tans.

Back on the Stingray, I turned left onto Town Line Road, detouring to a new house that resembled two old walls. A cross between an avant-garde castle and the back of a huge fireplace, it could have been built by masons from outer space. After staring in awe for a few minutes, I scooted around the corner and down Main Street, where, picking up speed on the straightaway by Wainscott Pond, I dreamed I was driver Mark Donohue attacking the Bridgehampton Race Circuit, a wicked serpentine of blind bends blocked by dunes.

At the eastern end of Main Street I sped across the finish line, the open gate of the Georgica Association, a colony founded in the 1880s by wealthy, sweaty Manhattanites seeking free air conditioning from summer sea breezes. I cycled through a forest seemingly imported from the Adirondacks; past the coved creeks of Georgica Pond, a tidal swimming pool for the likes of Carlos Montoya, the famous flamenco guitarist; around the softball field and former golf link where I turned double plays with my father; along the tennis courts where Dad hustled me in the shadow of a windmill moved from Montauk and Wainscott; over the speed bumps that made me a daredevil; through the prairie meadow that made me a naturalist; past a grove of wind-gnarled trees where I camped and fell asleep to the ocean's whispering hiss.

Back outside the association's entrance I zipped by a Kentucky antebellum mansion owned by cosmetics queen Estee Lauder; buttonhooked right onto Wainscott Stone Road, where actor Elliott Gould rented a house to escape the pressure of "M*A*S*H" fame; hung a left onto Wainscott North West Road, nicknamed "Turtle Road" for the turtles that waddled from the woods during rains, and hung another left onto Roxbury Lane, passing steeply slanted houses called saltboxes, built in the sixties by Wesley D. Miller, a real-estate cowboy with a 10-gallon hat. I turned right onto Foxcroft Lane, a major artery in the Miller-developed Westwoods and Wainscott's best playground. There I shot the shit with my best friend Mike Raffel, fellow baseball nut, rock 'n' roll guru and guardian of The Forum, a street basketball court with Wainscott's only street lamp south of the Montauk Highway, rigged on the sly by Mike's lineman father.

Behind the backboard was the modular, cabana-style house-studio of Jake Murray, my first writing and sex coach. That summer I basked in the reflected glory of his novel *The Devil*

*Walks on Water*, the semi-autobiographical, quasi-pornographic tale of the black sheep of a golden Irish-American clan during the 1938 hurricane, which tossed haves and have-nots into the same soup. I read the dirtiest bits—including a blow-by-blow of an unforgettable blowjob—on Jake's deck in seats from Ebbets Field, the late home of the late Brooklyn Dodgers, source of Jake's great ecstasy and greater misery.

My 4.3-mile mail call ended with a swing around the block to Whitney Lane, where my six-year-old sister Meg was playing with Clayton, Whitley and Douglas Kaufman, keeping the boys at bay by whimsically changing the rules of their games, shouting "Red Light!" when it was really green. I parked the Stingray on our lawn, which was cluttered with baseballs, footballs and croquet balls, and entered our two-year-old New England–Long Island Colonial. I kissed Mom, who was making jam from strawberries we picked along Main Street, and made a date with Dad to play baseball in the backyard, me pitching to him from a mound he built from dirt, sand and bricks.

My parents didn't care that their 11-year-old son had transformed a 20-minute trip into a 90-minute trek. In the anything-goes, everything-is-possible summer of 1969 they trusted Wainscott as a safe, stimulating, sanctified sanctuary. They knew it was my Woodstock, my moonwalk, mine.

Actually, I thought I owned the entire South Fork from 1967 to 1972, the years we lived on Whitney Lane. The Long Island Automotive Museum in Southampton, a Quonset hut with three bays, was my candy store for vintage vehicles, including a bullet-pierced 1933 Pierce Silver Arrow owned by Al Capone. The Penny

Henry Austin "Austie" Clark Jr., proprietor of the Long Island Automotive Museum in Southampton, pops a wheelie in a funny car made of odd parts from old vehicles, including a late 1920s Model T Ford. *(Photo courtesy of Walter McCarthy)*

Candy Shop in Water Mill was my pit stop for wax lips, chalky cigarettes and other sweets that turned kids into adults and adults into kids. At the Bridgehampton Race Circuit I fell for fiberglass spaceships hurtling at 170 mph; at the Hamptons Drive-In in Bridgehampton I fell for racing films starring Steve McQueen and Paul Newman, both of whom raced "The Bridge."

Sagaponack was the summer retreat of writer Truman Capote, who taught me that words can thrill like Christmas gifts and who gave my mother another sort of thrilling gift. A former pharmacy in East Hampton housed *The Star*, a weekly newspaper that groomed and willed me to become a journalist with panoramic, probing stories about fierce characters like Big Edie and Little Edie Beale, a mother-daughter tag team of aristocratic anarchists. Grey Gardens, their ramshackle-to-feral estate in East Hampton, pissed off their posh neighbors, triggered a class war heard 'round the world and made a financial angel of their notorious relation, Jacqueline Bouvier Kennedy Onassis. The Edies could have been invented by Capote or Westhampton Beach resident Charles Addams, the gloriously ghoulish cartoonist who could have invented the sinfully outrageous Capote.

This soulful amusement park was supervised by my parents, who spent precious little time by the ocean while growing up on different sides of the Atlantic. My father was a Mennonite minister's son from Easton, Pa., an ambitious advertising manager for a Manhattan magazine that covered the media business, a handsome Marlon Brando lookalike who invaded high society by playing squash, singing barbershop and schmoozing. My mother was a nurse's daughter from the London suburb of Palmers Green, a former telephone operator for the Queen Elizabeth I cruise ship, a brunette beauty who was fairly shy and cautious—except when she danced to a big band.

Patricia Cleversley and Larry Gehman met in 1957 through a mutual friend, a former U.S. Army soldier stationed in London during World War II. Their first date was a baseball game at the Polo Grounds in Manhattan; my very English mother wore white gloves and had no clue what Willie Mays was doing in center field. Six weeks later they married in the seaside town of Wildwood, N.J., where my father's minister brother-in-law was stationed. They began their life together in Manhattan, where I was born in 1958. That summer I made my South Fork debut in a rented railroad cottage in Hampton Bays, a few miles east of Westhampton Beach, where my father rented other cottages with other eligible bachelors and popularized volleyball by the ocean.

My parents settled me in the Westchester County suburb of New Rochelle, a half-hour train ride from Grand Central Station and the future locale of "The Dick Van Dyke Show" (I bet I was the only kid living in New Rochelle who didn't know that Laura and Rob Petrie lived in New Rochelle). After my sister arrived in 1962, Dad and Mom leased a roomier summer house in Quogue, another one of Dad's Hamptons haunts. We were there in 1966 when he bought the Gehmans' first piece of East End real estate, a half acre on Whitney Lane in Wainscott, across the street from a new home built by Bob and Jane Kaufman, his singing buddies. Dad purchased the property without telling Mom, an early sign of big trouble around the bend.

On this woodsy lot, in a relatively new, thoroughly middle-class neighborhood, my parents built a four-bedroom, two-bath home, converting a garage into a sunken family room with a two-way fireplace. House and land cost them $21,000, a king's ransom for a couple with two kids, two residences and an annual income under $30,000. Those who know even a little bit about the Hamptons know that $21,000 is chump change in today's ridiculously ritzy real-estate market. If you're lucky, it will buy you a two-month summer rental on the north, or wrong, side of the Montauk Highway.

Like virtually every adult from the suburbs or city, my parents had more fun on the South Fork. They lounged on the beach, played tennis and golf, had date nights with their underage kids while watching R-rated films at the drive-in. They hosted parties starring my father's singing and my mother's beef bourguignon and attended parties starring celebrities. It was at an Amagansett wingding that I met Fred Gwynne, who played the lovably goofy, green-faced Herman on "The Munsters." I lamented to him that school bullies called me "Herman" because the large birthmark on my neck reminded them of the electrical bolts on Mr. Munster's neck. Shuttering the sun with his 6-foot-5 self, Gwynne smiled and said softly: "Leave it to me—I've got something that will shut them up." Within the week he sent me an autographed photograph of himself as Herman. My enemies shut up for good when they read the inscription: "To Geoff—my second favorite Herman."

While the South Fork was paradise for me, it became less so for my parents. Worried about paying two mortgages on time, they never fully relaxed in that adult oasis. Over six years they were increasingly divided by my father's boozing, his investment failures, their polar-opposite personalities. Simply put, Dad was a social bulldozer; Mom cleaned up his messes.

My family wasn't the only one flattened on the East End, much of which is bevel level. Too much boredom aggravated alcoholism and mental illness; too much freedom accelerated divorce and suicide. Lives eroded like dunes and duneside lawns, which disappeared into the sea despite ugly concrete jetties that turned beaches into Normandy battlegrounds. Falling potato prices forced farmers to sell acres to house developers who spoiled lovely fields with absurdly angled Rubik's Cube boxes. Rising property prices shoved the middle class off their comfortable island.

I was sheltered from these storms until the summer of 1972, when my father abruptly shut the door to my heaven on earth—

with my toes still on the saddle. By then the damage was done, thankfully. In six years the South Fork had significantly stretched my mind, my heart, my vision. I had learned lifelong lessons about beauty and cruelty, humility and decency. I had grown up, and out.

# Keys to the Kingdom

The Whitney Lane Bike Gang, July 1970. Clayton Kaufman is at far left, Meg Gehman fourth from left, Whitley Kaufman at center, Douglas Kaufman fourth from right. *(Photo courtesy of Clay Kaufman)*

# THE WESTWOODS

Did you ever have a summer when the worst thing that happened to you was repeatedly stubbing your bare toe on the street? In Wainscott I had five straight summers like that, when nothing, not even the agonizing, hop-till-you-drop pain of tar toe, kept me from being a capitalist of fun.

We all took advantage of natural advantages. We fished in the Atlantic Ocean, crabbed in Georgica Pond, hunted for ducks around Wainscott Pond. We played volleyball on Beach Lane beach, hockey on a frozen potato field at the corner of Main Street and Sayre's Path, baseball with small potatoes gleaned from the

Meg Gehman is chauffeured by family friend Jane Dickinson in the Gehman backyard in Wainscott, September 1968. *(Gehman Family Collection)*

fall harvest. Back then farmers often ignored trespassers, so we weren't afraid of being chased by car, tractor or gun. We were permitted to do pretty much everything and anything because no permit was required.

The bull's eye of fun was the six-block area around our house in the Westwoods. Filled with scrub oaks, the woods were perfect for catching frogs, building forts, riding bicycles, jumping motorcycles, playing hide-and-seek. Screens of pines served as screens for more illicit activities: smoking, kissing, copping a feel. It was behind a stand of pines behind our house on Whitney Lane that I buried a stash of plastic-wrapped skin magazines hidden from everyone, even Mike Raffel, my *Playboy*-reading pal.

The straight, flat roads in the Westwoods were perfect for bike skidding, my favorite game. We'd race our Stingrays from the end of Whitney Lane, hit top speed at the three-quarter mark and slam the brakes at the thickest portion of a thin coat of sand, using it as a slick to make rubber burns longer and nastier. We'd measure the black lightning marks with our feet, hollering and whooping as we determined who would be that day's Evel Knievel Jr. Recklessness was rampant because extra points were given for zigzagging into intersections and ramming into sandy berms.

Every neighborhood has a Kid Central. We were lucky enough to have three gang hangouts. Our property was a haven for relatively calm fun. Our big basement was ideal for ping-pong and darts. Our large, grassy yard was ideal for baseball and football, badminton and croquet, hide-and-seek and red light/green light.

Diagonally across Whitney Lane was another entertainment emporium. Here, in and around a rustic rancher with a breezeway, Bob and Jane Kaufman let their sons Clayton, Whitley and Douglas do everything they couldn't do in their cramped Manhattan apartment. In the city the boys were scolded for playing ball indoors. In the country they were encouraged to romp inside and out.

When it came to fun, the Kaufman kids were venture capitalists. They organized bicycle races for little and big kids, two and three wheels. They raced lobsters on the porch, with the winner losing and being tossed into a pot of boiling water. Even garbage pickups were exciting affairs, stirring the boys to fill their Tonka trucks with newspapers and washcloths.

Doug, Whit and Clay were spoiled by their parents, who grew up in wealthy New York families whose wealth was depressed by the Depression. Bob, a copy editor for *Newsweek* magazine and a doctoral student in English, was a playful, mindful teacher. He took the boys fishing, sailing and camping, sleeping alone in a front-yard tent after his cold, itchy kids bolted indoors one by one. He expanded their imaginations by acting Sherlock Holmes mysteries by the fire and studying animal tracks on the beach. A caring naturalist, he made sure they returned turtles to the road where they had been found, pointing in their original directions.

Bob could be stern, especially when swamped by work and school work. His eyes would burn behind his academic glasses, his owlish face would twitch, his fairly high voice would get higher and louder. Jane, on the other hand, pretty much always remained merry. She made sure the boys had birthday parties in the city and country, helped them tend their vegetable plots in the backyard garden, kept them active with games, songs and field trips. Driving them to tennis lessons in the Georgica Association, she allowed them to dangle their legs from the tailgate of the family station wagon. When the Ford Falcon hit the speed bumps, and the kids screamed with joy, she became giddy, her smiling eyes becoming slits. Back then she had no worries that anyone would call the cops or child welfare.

Jane was a fascinating mix of order and disorder. Pipe-cleaner thin, with a nearly squeaky voice and bobbed brown-red hair, she was an athletic version of Jacqueline Bouvier before she married John F. Kennedy. Her dinners were casual picnics. She always seemed to serve clam dip with Fritos, blue fish or fish sticks, corn on the cob and nutless brownies. Her housekeeping was nearly disastrous. The living room was a steeplechase of toys. The kitchen had as many dishes on counters as in cupboards. Laundry was piled on tables, floors, even the player piano that Doug Kaufman played by hitting the foot pedals with his hands because he was too short to finger the keys.

Jane kept a messy home partly to rebel against a stiflingly neat childhood. She was reminded of her white-glove youth every time her mother, Meme, visited the Whitney Lane house in her white gloves. A kind soul with a strong streak of Southern gentility, Meme slept in a bedroom painted blue, her favorite color and Jane's least favorite color. It was a daughter's concession to a mother who basically bought the daughter's retreat.

While Jane kept a messy home, she kept a neat neighborhood. She was Whitney Lane's resident photographer, counselor and den mother. She could turn dessert into an international adventure, speaking with her mother in basic French until her sons figured out the babble was really a sign to lobby her to go get ice cream.

"My mother was a laissez-faire homemaker," says Clay Kaufman with a laugh. "I have to give her credit, though. She spent tons of time reading and playing with us. She just made that her priority. It drove us crazy eventually because the house was a mess. But, then, she could just let us be kids, and that was priceless."

Over on Foxcroft Lane, across the woods from the Kaufmans' home, was the Westwoods community center. There were three reasons why the split level with aqua vinyl siding was a kid castle. One, Joe and Rosie Raffel's five children—Mike, Karen, Joey, Carol and Doreen—had tons of friends. Two, the Raffels operated Wainscott's only street basketball court, which had Wainscott's only street lamp south of the Montauk Highway and the East End's largest community bench—a telephone pole laid on its side. And, three, Rosie and Joe ran their home as a bed & breakfast & lunch & dinner & midnight snack. The front door opened so much it should have revolved.

On many summer nights the place was a mess hall. As many as 20 kids ate at the picnic table in the kitchen-dining room or on the floor in the adjacent living room. An excellent military/assembly-line cook, Rosie would make, say, stuffed peppers for the next night while everyone stuffed themselves with, say, stuffed shells. I'll always be in her debt for introducing me to the hearty, spicy pleasures of kielbasa, which she cooked mainly to please Joe, a Polish-American from Southampton, a Polish-American enclave.

Joe was a powerful presence: 6-foot-1 with a bullish build, big hands, a prominent nose and a handsomely craggy face. His hair was sharply parted; his voice foggy, froggy and booming; his grin "crooked, dopey and wise-ass," says Rosie, who fell for it hook, line and sinker. Extremely nice and surprisingly gentle, he raised rabbits, carved duck decoys and not only managed the local baseball team but bought its equipment, too.

What made Rosie and Joe's impressive generosity even more so is that they were chronically busy raising five youngsters. She waited tables, cleaned and cooked for a family in the Georgica Association, served as a bank secretary and bookkeeper. He worked every possible shift as a lineman for the Long Island Lighting Company. He was constantly on call to repair wires and poles knocked down by gale-force winds whipped by the sea. During emergencies he could work 16 hours straight.

Kids could make almost as much noise as they wanted in the Raffel house except when Joe was napping on the livingroom couch, recovering from a late shift or preparing for a double. Jolted from a deep sleep, he could become angry and intimidating. "You didn't want to wake him up from his nap," says Rosie. "Oh God, no. Unless you had a drink to give him when he woke up."

Rosie was a spunky Irish-American from Shelter Island and Sag Harbor. She was 5 feet tall with a rosy complexion, chipmunk cheeks, a chirpy voice and a rosy attitude. She was pretty cheery until you crossed her; then her shout could shake windows. Astrologists might attribute her temper to being born the day of the 1938 hurricane.

Rosie had the ESP of a psychic, the radar of a cop. She would interrupt whatever she was saying or doing when she saw smoke rising above the window above the front door. She knew that 9 times out of 10 she'd open the door and nab underage smokers. "They'd swear up and down it was their breath in the cold air, but you knew they were puffing away like chimneys," she says with a laugh. "And they'd ask: How come you know? And I'd say because I was that age once, too, and I was no angel. They couldn't trick a trickster."

The Raffel house tripled as a crash pad for tipsy, troubled children. Rosie gave them mattresses to sleep off hangovers and counseled them the way she was counseled by a girlfriend's mother after her father died when she was 14. "I always felt that kids had to have someone to talk to," she says. "They had to feel like they had a home in our house."

Actually, the entire Westwoods was a safe house. Car traffic was light, so you could run wild on the streets without worry. Crime was light, so you could keep your windows open at night without worry. Most parents were in their 20s or 30s and had at least two children, so you could almost always find a playmate, even in the dog days of November. Parents felt better knowing their kids were happy and secure outdoors, even in the deepest woods during the deepest dusk.

In addition to being a baby-boomer case study, the Westwoods was a protective melting pot. We lived around the corner from two lawyers, across the street from an accountant and next door to a gay antiques dealer. If we had a medical crisis, we could call on two nurses, one married to a surgeon. Crime was light largely because a detective lived a block from a retired New York City cop. A bicycle repairman kept us mobile and agile, essentials for any kid in any season. Two freelance writers for *The East Hampton Star* made our adventures more adventurous. They chronicled our softball games, our dog-and-pony shows, our free concert with

Paul McCartney from a house rented by his brother-in-law John Eastman, an entertainment lawyer plotting a post-Beatles empire.

What else could be better than having your ordinary deeds made extraordinary within the week, for the whole South Fork to read? I can't think of anything, except, perhaps, an entire summer without a single incident of tar toe.

# THE BEACH

Three things from my past are always present. One is pitching a baseball, which I did for 12 years and stopped too soon. Another is singing with my father, who was my first pitching coach and who died too soon. The last is exploring the 1,000 or so steps from Beach Lane beach to Georgica Pond, the first stretch of sand that taught me about beauty, cruelty and humility.

My day at Beach Lane beach typically began with a barrel roll down the dunes. In the old days it was a dramatic entrance for the benefit of friends and strangers; these days it's outlawed as a threat to the Piping Plover and the Least Tern, both endangered birds. After shaking sand from my swim trunks and shaking wits back into my head, I trudged across the ocean desert, building my calves 12 ways. If the sand was scalding, as it usually was in the middle of summer, I hopped, scooted and Indian rain danced, never caring how foolish I looked. No matter what the temperature, I dodged jagged tabs ripped from cans of beer and soda. There was no way in hell I was going to end a day at the beach before it started, with a bloody foot and a trip to the emergency room.

The next step was setting up camp, sometimes with weekend guests, more often with the Kaufmans, our Whitney Lane neighbors. After flinging down my towel and flip-flops, I dashed to the sea to join a brigade of body surfers. When I rode the waves right, I felt like a greased rocket. When the waves rode me wrong, I felt like a rag doll tossed in a washing machine. I can't count the number of times I tumbled head over ass, scraped rocks and shells, snorted water, saw stars and stripes, got sucked back to sea by a riptide, clawed the sand in desperation and imagined myself as shark food.

Dying in unimaginable agony, in front of my loved ones, was my greatest fear, a fear far greater than losing my parents or being kidnapped by the monster under my bed.

Luckily, I never needed rescuing. That was a minor miracle, considering the wicked undertow and the complete absence of lifeguards at Beach Lane beach. One man wasn't so lucky. In his early 50s and overweight, he drifted far from shore, developed cramps in his legs and abdomen, and sank like an anchor. A team of volunteer lifeguards pulled him back to the beach unconscious, bright red from being raked by stones and light blue from lack of oxygen. Revived by CPR, he shivered and coughed, spouting

Kilkare, the 19th-century mansion moored like a ship on the dune between Beach Lane beach and Georgica Pond, has been a Hamptons mascot for everything from De Beers diamonds to a James Patterson novel. *(Photo courtesy of Doug Benedict)*

water from nose, mouth and, I swear, ears. Scared shitless by his near-death experience, I stayed out of the water the rest of the day, an eternity for a boy with gills.

Beach Lane beach forced me to respect the ocean as king, queen and bastard goddess. It also proved that a beach is a superior sandbox for all sorts of sports. Flying a kite. Tossing a football. Spiking a volleyball. Flinging a Frisbee—with humans and dogs. Doing all the above to show off for sexy girls, my fantasy subjects while lying on a blanket after a swim, another favorite recreation. There was something exotic and erotic about being a tuning fork for wind, waves, seagulls, voices, radio songs and other white noises.

Every day my bliss was interrupted by lunch, a necessary evil. The only time it was entertaining was the time my sister Meg strolled from stranger to stranger, asking for something better to eat than egg-salad sandwiches. Devastatingly cute and downright foxy, she received hot dogs, chicken legs and a bellyache.

Lunch was followed by the dreaded digestion break, ordered by my mother to prevent us from cramping while swimming on a full stomach. I filled the void by combing the beach for pieces of animal-shaped driftwood and shards of colored glass, frosted remnants of bottles that farmers dumped under dunes. I pondered such existential questions as "Why don't I ever cut my foot on pop tops?" as I flipped horseshoe crabs with a stick, poked their innards to see them squirm, and pondered such nonexistential questions as "Wouldn't this shell be a terrific helmet on Halloween?"

Along the way I dreamed of living in a pair of noble houses, the only homes between Beach Lane beach and Georgica Pond. Parked by the Beach Lane parking lot was a 1920s Georgian mansion with white-painted bricks, four chimneys and a tennis court fenced by a thicket of pines. Once owned by a Texas oilman who hunted big game for a natural-history museum, it was owned by John Nagel, a mysterious South Fork newcomer married to a soap heiress. A fish out of water, the house seemed too elegant, too permanent, for the dunes. It belonged not in Wainscott but in a suburb like New Rochelle.

A few football fields east was a nineteenth-century shingled mansion moored above the dunes like a ship in a slip. A covered, second-floor porch was built by a dock carpenter, who supported the balcony and a small crow's-nest extension with 10 arches, or ship's knees. Finished in 1881 for a charter member of the Georgica Association, the 40-window house was bought in 1968 by Charles Benedict, the son of a hotel chef in Southern California, a Wall Street investment banker married to a member of the Steinway piano dynasty. Officially known as Kilkare and unofficially known as "The Tara of Wainscott," it's long been a Hamptons mascot, advertising everything from De Beers diamonds to a novel co-written by James Patterson. In the film "Eternal Sunshine of the Spotless Mind" it's a refuge for refugees from a memory-erasing clinic.

Back then the Benedict and Nagel properties were in danger of becoming sea toys. Both estates had lost large chunks of yard and dune to nasty storms and sand blocked by jetties on nearby East Hampton beaches. These north-south groins were erected in the sixties by the U.S. Army Corps of Engineers at the request of such power brokers as Juan Trippe—commercial-aviation pioneer, chairman of Pan Am Airways and owner of a mansion overlooking the Atlantic and Georgica Pond. Before the Army came to his rescue, Trippe tried to stall erosion below his property with a jetty of junked cars. The auto graveyard riled beach lovers much more than, say, a reef of rusty Christmas trees.

Like Trippe, Nagel and Benedict tried to tame nature and finagle fate. First they hired a company to bury in the sand under their estates a barricade of chained cesspool rings filled with rubble.

Eroding sand exposed part of a jetty installed to prevent sand from eroding on the stretch from Beach Lane beach to Georgica Pond. *(Photo courtesy of Clay Kaufman)*

The experiment failed when the concrete cracked and the rings were exposed by wind and water. By the fall of 1969 Nagel's brick mansion had lost 65 feet of lawn, leaving the house only 13 feet from the beach and perilously close to an unholy salt-water baptism. It was a far cry from the mansion's 1,000 feet of backyard when it was completed for banker Lansing MacVicker, who lost his fortune and his Beach Lane Shangri-La to the 1929 stock-market tsunami.

Benedict then erected his own personal jetty, an assortment of 20 or so concrete cylinders below Kilkare. In April 1969 the groin generated a dispute over who really owned the beach. According to an eyewitness (an Air Force lieutenant), Richard Fabricant, a lawyer who lived around the corner from us on Roxbury Lane, was sitting on the jetty, watching his children play on the beach, when Benedict ordered him to leave "my property." Fabricant allegedly declined to budge; Benedict allegedly fetched an air rifle from Kilkare and hit Fabricant in the face with the butt. After his chin and lip were stitched up, Fabricant filed a complaint against Benedict, who was arrested while mowing his shrinking lawn.

Fabricant declines to discuss his Benedict altercation. He does say he thoroughly enjoyed his time in Wainscott, which lasted from 1968 to 1978. He and his wife Florence, now a food writer for *The New York Times*, ate freshly picked corn and freshly caught crabs, let their kids frolic all over the Westwoods, and considered their compact contemporary house a peace retreat. Shocked by Robert Kennedy's assassination in June 1968, the Fabricants drove from their Manhattan apartment with the car radio off to spend a weekend in the Roxbury Lane woods trying to recover from the second murder of an American civil-rights leader in three months.

Benedict is dead, as are his wife, Julia, and their oldest son, Brad. Their surviving child, Doug, insists his father preached nonviolence to his kids. "He used to tell us that the best way to win a fight is to never have a fight," says Doug Benedict, who adds that his dad kept his antique guns, including a Revolutionary War blunderbuss, locked in a Kilkare case. "Although, if you're forced into a corner, and you have to fight, just make sure you're the last man standing."

The same year Benedict and Nagel joined forces yet again to save their estates from vanishing down Davy Jones' drain. They spent $20,000 on a bigger, uglier barricade of reinforced concrete cylinders connected by steel rods. Placed near the western border of Nagel's property, the groin ran 150 feet from the Atlantic to the Beach Lane parking lot. A sort of Normandy wall, it immediately became a battleground of private-public rights. Verbal assaults were reported dutifully and wryly by *The East Hampton Star*, which has been covering real-estate storms and beach wars since 1885. At one point the weekly paper joked that locals blamed the Nagel-Benedict reef for everything from inflation to the golden nematode, a potato fungus. The fungus began withering in July 1971, when a Supreme Court justice in Riverhead ordered the jetty removed because it endangered bathers and boaters.

Benedict eventually waved the white flag, declaring nature the winner. He let his dune become a cliff and watched as Kilkare's neighbor, the Georgica Association's bath house, was moved back from the beach for the third time in two decades. This option wasn't available to Nagel, who couldn't afford to jack up and haul a house made of bricks. Insured against fire but not erosion, he reportedly paid two men $30,000 to burn his mansion so he could collect a $240,000 insurance policy. In December 1973 the alleged arsonists were arrested while carrying gasoline cans into the Beach Lane building. The Town of East Hampton designated the house a hazard and in December 1974 torched it, this time legally, before the entire place fell into the sea and became a giant jetty. Broke and broken, Nagel later killed himself in a Baltimore hotel.

The beach war created a strange paradox. As the dunes shrank, stories about them swelled. Old timers recalled the days of double dunes with triple roles. The giant sandbanks offered great views of the church steeple in Bridgehampton, five miles away. Hollows in the interior dune served as a semi-private chamber for changing clothes. They were an even better place for fooling around, a custom quaintly known as "fogging up the windows."

Some of this bygone romance lingered in the 80-foot-high dunes in Napeague, a desert-like hamlet between Amagansett and Montauk. The sandbanks changed shape and size constantly, sculpted in a wide-open, wildly atmospheric basin between ocean and bay. The Gehman and Kaufman kids treated them as tidal waves of sand, perfect for rolling and surfing. We sat on them as twilight became dusk and dusk became night, eating hot dogs cooked on a hibachi fired by burning newspaper and listening to ghost stories. We had no idea we were sitting near a ghostly set for "The Sheik," a 1921 silent film starring Rudolph Valentino as a shamanic lover.

Napeague was breathtakingly mercurial; Georgica Pond was sublimely mercurial. The 290-acre pond has long been the South Fork's most versatile, vibrant inland waterway. It's a marine estuary. A freshwater coastal lagoon. A home to spotted turtles and diamond-back terrapins. A border between the Town and the Village of East Hampton. A protective barrier and picturesque coast for the Georgica Association. A swimming pool and status symbol for such mover-shakers as domestic diva Martha Stewart and filmmaker-impresario Steven Spielberg, whose movie "Catch Me If You Can" features Pan Am, Juan Trippe's old airline.

For me and countless other kids, Georgica was an incredibly seductive oasis. Because it had no big waves and no riptides, we swam, sailed and caught crabs without fear of drowning or becoming shark bait. I especially loved the way it constantly changed personality. During heavy storms it overflowed onto the beach, shaping the sandbar into a levee of streams. During droughts it became a brackish chocolate soup and a mud flat, allowing me to walk near its middle for a better view of a mass of crooked inlets and fancy properties. The fanciest was The Creeks, a legendary home, arboretum and sculpture park. The owner, surrealist artist Alfonso Ossorio, ran a fabled museum-gallery-salon for famous friends. One night a typically plastered Jackson Pollock crashed a party and attacked the keys of a piano with an ice pick. He wasn't making performance art.

Seeking peace, Ossorio turned the pond into yet another war zone. In 1970 he installed a 300-foot-long cement wall to protect The Creeks from the annual Georgica flood that turned the estate into a swamp. Criticized for spoiling the pond's wild beauty, Ossorio responded by decorating the wall with his wacky totems of found objects, many painted red, white and blue, all symbolic raised middle fingers. These "conglomerations" probably spooked the spirit of the pond's namesake, Jeorgkee, a seventeenth-century Native American who hunted whales with white men.

Georgica was a partner in one of my all-time favorite beach rituals. Every spring and fall the Town of East Hampton bulldozed, or "let," a north-south channel on the beach that connected the pond to the ocean. The "gut" transformed the pond into a temporary lake, harbor and bay. More important, it drained basements, refreshed the stagnant lagoon with salt water, and provided sea food for striped bass, spawning crabs and other sea food. Shaped by the ocean into a sandy canyon, it became a wet dream for sportsmen, who caught fish and crabs in a very big barrel.

To me, the stretch from the pond to Beach Lane beach was never more magical than during early evening from late summer to early fall. Fading light created dramatic 12-foot shadows. The setting sun tinted the sand a gentle pink. Ocean reflections transformed clouds into fleecy tire tracks and Kilkare's windows into amber eyes. It was the best time to forget everything but the wind, think yet not think, creep toward that nirvana of just being.

# THE SETTLEMENT

I received only one shock during the making of this book, not a bad record considering it took nearly 20 years to research, report, write, edit and think. The shock came in an e-mail from a fellow former Wainscotteer who accused me, very gently, of being what I wasn't: a rich kid. She assumed, quite politely, that I was born to the manor simply because I played tennis in tennis whites in the Georgica Association, a colony with more than a few white-linen bluebloods.

I wish I had told her then what I'm telling her now. That my family was almost as middle class as hers. That my father had neither the money nor the pedigree to own or even rent a home in Georgica. That I lived how the other half lives for three summers, three to 12 hours a day, thanks to a fluke of friendship.

The Gehmans were associate members of Georgica only because we were endorsed by Bill Noble, a member of my father's barbershop quartet, an association resident and a great-grandson of Walter Edwards, one of the settlement's charter members. In 1881 Edwards bought 20-plus acres from Georgica's founding entrepreneur, William H. S. Wood, who made a fortune publishing educational books and *The Medical Record*, a weekly journal. Later a leader of the YMCA and the American Bible Society, Wood decided it would be good medicine to create a summer retreat from noisy, sweaty Manhattan for himself and his wealthy friends. Among the privileged pals was Walter Edwards, his lawyer.

"They wanted to be cooled by ocean breezes in their jackets and high collars," says Noble, a Manhattan native whose father was a Union Carbide lawyer. "They wanted a place where they could get a good night's sleep in peace."

In 1882 Walter Edwards made his mark on the association by building its first landmark: a shingled, ship-shaped, duneside mansion with a glorious view of the ocean. The 40-window summer cottage was called Kilkare, a bastard Celtic contraction for "kill all care." "It's a frighteningly Victorian name," says Noble. "Perhaps my great-grandmother thought it was cute." Adds his brother Tim: "Gloppy, sentimental nicknames for summer houses were the rage in the Victorian era, I'm told. Like Shangri-La."

Three years later Edwards began building a family compound, a settlement within the Settlement. His brother Charlie moved into a smaller shingled house with a wraparound porch and seven gables about 260 steps below Kilkare. Located in a sweeping field full of goldenrod, it was named Solidago, Linnean for goldenrod.

It was here that the Noble brothers escaped sweaty, noisy Manhattan with their sisters and parents. As a kid Bill Noble escaped adult supervision by reading trashy novels in the loft of Kilkare's barn, which once housed cars, farm equipment and carriages that picked up visitors at Wainscott's train station, now a duneside sanctuary in Sagaponack. Around 1960 he received the barn and nearly three acres of land as a wedding gift from his mother, who received the property as payment for lending money to her down-and-out brother. Then a marketing official for a valve manufacturer, Noble designed and converted the barn into a marvelously rustic, elegant home for himself, his copywriter wife Joyce and their kids, Nick and Maggie, who were born, like the Gehman kids, in New York Hospital in Manhattan. There were six bedrooms, four baths and a two-story tower, once a windmill that pumped water to the Kilkare estate. The tower became magical on stormy days, when we took turns spinning a spinning wheel, dreaming it was the wheel of a ship tossed by a turbulent sea.

The Noble house was long, humped and topped by a whale weathervane. I was a whale nut at the time, so I thought the whole place resembled a shingled, beached leviathan. The tower was the fin. The living-room beams were the ribs. The jaw—or part of it—was in the cellar, a relic from an actual whale found on the grounds.

Whalebone Manor was moored 300 steps from the sea in an oceanic meadow, a prairie labyrinth of goldenrod, honeysuckle, thorny shrubs and meandering paths. My favorite refuge was a grove of Shad trees sculpted by the wind into gnarly, giant witch fingers. Nick Noble and I camped at night in a tent in this "Where the Wild Things Are" haven. We ate peanut-butter-and-jelly sandwiches and read comic books by flashlight. We felt completely, blissfully independent, even though his parents were only a stone's throw away. We were lulled to sleep by the crashing waves, which the dunes muted to a hushed roar. Five decades later, we both agree there is no more seductive siren than the sea.

Nick and I learned to play tennis on Georgica's clay courts on land donated by his great-grandfather. Our teacher was Virginia Turner, winner of the national 18-and-under doubles championship with Shirley Fry (Irvin), who later won all four Grand Slam singles tournaments and topped the world's female players. Married to a librarian who opened libraries in Bangladesh, Turner was whippet-slim, leather-tanned and drill-sergeant tough. She smoked Viking cigarillos as she instructed us to wear whites, be on time and mind our manners. We had no idea she had a nobler mission. "My mother used tennis as a social organizer," says her son, James, "as a way of keeping the association from being too gossipy or backbiting, to keep people as good neighbors."

I became a bad neighbor when Turner wasn't around. She surely would have dressed me down for drinking water from tennis-ball cans. For some reason I wasn't bothered by the metallic taste and the fuzzy aftertaste of the water, which I cranked from an old iron pump by the courts. I wasn't even bothered by the slightly acrid smell of pesticides drifting from a potato field behind the fence.

That fence was my wall of shame, the backboard for rackets flung in frustration during painfully lopsided games with my father. It was in Georgica that I discovered Dad was a tennis hustler. That is, he hustled me over every goddamned inch of the court with topspin forehands, backhand slices and delicately arcing, annoyingly out-of-reach lobs. He insisted the tricky shots would make me a fiercer competitor; he never admitted they helped him save his energy while recovering from a hangover. When I yelled at him for yelling at me, he placed his racket on the court and walked away. His early exit pissed me off me even more, compelling me to make a racket with the fence.

Dad and I behaved better during the association's softball games, held on Sundays on an oblong oval, a kind of village green. I played second base, he played first base, and we were quite the father-son double-play bare-footed combo. Even though Dad was in his early 40s, which was ancient in my book, he was exceptionally agile. He stretched full out to scoop up bouncing throws, slapped singles through seeing-eye holes and beat out drag bunts. Leave it to my hyper-competitive father to bunt during gentlemanly contests on the Sabbath.

The softball games usually matched teams of association members against teams of nonmembers. The custom was one of many ways the Settlement tried to remain friendly with the rest of Wainscott. Over 13 decades the two communities have bonded

In the 1940s the Georgica Association tennis courts were joined by a windmill erected in the 19<sup>th</sup> century elsewhere in Wainscott. *(Photo by Bill Hayward)*

over everything from fishing to farming, square dancing to rum running.

It was William Wood who started the concept of Georgica as a kind of democratic kingdom. The association's patriarch had a strange sense of noblesse oblige. As president of the Bowery Savings Bank he loaned money to immigrants. As Georgica president he donated Beach Lane to local fishermen, mainly to keep them off the Settlement's private lane to the ocean. Yet he instituted Georgica's code of respect for the Osborns, an original Wainscott clan who sold him 50 of the association's 137 acres. The code meant that Elisha Osborn, born the same year as the association, could be eulogized by Settlement leaders as an all-time go-to good guy:

"His tomatoes and the eggs from his chicken-house were apt to be large. His heart was larger still." The code also meant that David Osborn, Elisha's nephew, could attend Settlement cocktail parties and date Settlement girls even though he lived on the family farm on Main Street, a fraction of a mile from the association's entrance.

No wonder David Osborn regards Georgica with fond wonder. "There was a time when I thought I wouldn't mind if it wasn't there," says the retired farmer, who still lives on Main Street. "The last 20 to 30 years I've looked at it as a unique organization of families trying to maintain a certain social status. I often think of what three generations of Osborns would have done without the Georgica Association: it certainly added spice to our lives. It's like being a Communist: you're allowed to keep a church as a museum. Well, that's our museum."

Georgica was, in fact, a lively museum of living archaeology. The north lawn of Kilkare once contained a baseball diamond, complete with mound and chicken-wire backstop. The softball field was part of an extinct nine-hole golf course, most of which ran through members' properties; it was nicknamed, naturally, "The Missing Link." The windmill by the tennis courts was moved from Montauk after a 1940s subscription crusade led by George Wilson Pierson, a Yale history chairman who inherited his association home from his mother. Pierson, who wrote a pamphlet on the Settlement's first 68 years, wasn't trying to make Georgica some sort of South Fork heritage park. He simply believed the windmill deserved to be closer to its original site, a hill between Main Street and Wainscott Hollow Road, near the general store. He also endorsed its use as living quarters for the Settlement's lifeguard.

Like any living museum, Georgica exhibited many intriguing specimens. Goodhue Livingston Jr., who lived in an elegant Colonial overlooking Georgica Pond and the softball field, was the child of an architect who designed the Hayden Planetarium. He received a Croix de Guerre for World War I bravery and served New York City's planning commission from 1945 to 1960. As Mayor Fiorello La Guardia's executive secretary in 1944–1945, he coordinated patriotic rallies in Central Park attended by more than a million spectators. His fourth wife, Dorothy, also came from hearty stock. Her father, Albert Abraham Michelson, was the first American to receive the Nobel Prize for physics, an honor she discussed in her biography of her dad.

A more powerful power broker lived inland, some 240 steps from Solidago, in a fairly modest Japanese-style chalet. Alfred

The author camped at Whalebone Manor, the Noble family home in the Georgica Association built around an old barn, topped by a whale weathervane and resembling a wooden leviathan. *(Photo courtesy of Doug Benedict)*

Hayes directed the Federal Reserve Bank of New York, the largest of 12 district units. A former Rhodes Scholar (his thesis was on the Federal Reserve), the global financial wizard helped convince international bankers in the mid-sixties to bolster the value of the distressed British pound sterling. Like Goodhue Livingston, he had a wife with a fabled father. Vilma "Bebbe" Chalmers Hayes was the daughter of Thomas Hardie Chalmers, a Metropolitan Opera baritone, director of silent-film comedy shorts ("The Sex Life of the Polyp") and an actor on Broadway ("Death of a Salesman") and TV ("Mister Peepers"). Quite theatrical herself, Bebbe (pronounced "Beb-BUH") played the role of Settlement enforcer. She demanded that strangers declare their affiliation, and she rapped a cane on the side of a van to protest the delivery of a catered beach dinner. Meals on Georgica Beach, she ardently believed, should be made only by Georgica cooks.

Georgica's most colorful character didn't even live there. A resident of Sayre's Path, Pete Morrison was a chauffeur for James Hendrick, a State Department lawyer who lived near the Settlement's entrance in a cruise ship of a mansion. Morrison had the bushy eyebrows and piercingly dark eyes of comedian George Jessel, regularly swam in the ocean at 5 a.m., and reportedly became wealthy by listening in the driver's seat to stock tips traded in the backseat. A native of the Outer Hebrides, he celebrated his Scottish heritage by marching in an ancestral kilt and playing the bagpipes during birthday, cocktail and D-Day parties. Fueled by Scotch, he became a Celtic comic. "I'm Bobby Burns on the bridge of Leath," he crowed in his thick burr. "I've lost the key to my arse, so I'm shittin' through my teeth!"

The association's most renowned resident was a professional entertainer. Flamenco guitarist Carlos Montoya was an international celebrity for his fiery, sparkling, quicksilver runs shaded by guttural vocals, clicking heels and other elements of his Spanish gypsy heritage. Starting in 1948, he elevated a mostly peasant instrument to a solo classical star. In 1966 he made his star shine brighter by premiering a flamenco orchestral suite.

Montoya lived in Georgica because his wife had summered there with her parents in a cottage on the Hendrick estate. Sally McLean Montoya, a former Spanish dancer, was the child of a U.S. ambassador to Spain and a descendant of the founders of McLean, Va. Her prominent father was none too pleased when his teen-aged daughter fell for Montoya, who as a teen spent most of his café wages buying wine for customers, angling for better tips. "My father's whole family was out making music," says Allan Montoya, son of Carlos and Sally, "or dancing or stealing horses, literally."

According to his son, Montoya treasured Georgica as a retreat from the pressures of living out of suitcases and soloing with a notoriously difficult instrument. The association "was my father's touchstone—that was where he felt the best," says Allan. "He could take his walks around the property, maybe down to the water. Or he could sit in his chair and do nothing. He had no worries."

Montoya was comfortable enough in Georgica to play a very private recital in the living room at Solidago for the Nobles' father, who had been too ill to attend the guitarist's concert at Carnegie Hall. Montoya was so settled, in fact, that he built the Settlement's first thoroughly modern house, which had a pink stucco façade and a living room on the second floor, to maximize a view of Georgica Pond. According to Allan Montoya, the mildly radical house was criticized mildly by the association's gabled, gambrel-roofed, shingled-ship traditionalists. "At that time everybody was really quiet about their social status," he says. "Nobody was tooting their own horn. Everybody knew who everybody was, and nobody had anything to sell."

Actually, it was Allan Montoya who caused the biggest ruckus when he turned Georgica's bucolic lanes into a motorcycle speedway. In 1965 the Settlement's leaders installed speed bumps to slow him down and restore the almighty peace. Little did they know the obstacles would quickly become his opportunities. "It took me 30 seconds to realize, oh my God, I could go flying!" he says with a laugh. "Well, I owned those speed bumps; they were *mine*."

What Montoya calls "Mexican road signs" symbolized Georgica's first era of significant change. In the sixties association leaders introduced tennis lessons and reintroduced Sunday softball games to satisfy a swarm of children. These baby boomers routinely disobeyed rules intended to keep the Settlement civil and genteel. They ran amuck at July 4 windmill parties and Monday night beach bonfires. They made the bathhouse a wee-hour club for booze, drugs and sex. They risked life and limb slamming speed bumps on bikes, motorbikes and station-wagon tailgates.

If Georgica had a kid castle, it was Kilkare, the Settlement's highest house. The mansion's owners, Charlie and Julia Benedict, both in their 30s and beach lovers, encouraged their sons Brad and Doug to catch crabs with fish heads and blast sand castles with firecrackers. Kilkare was the premiere site, and star, of Nick Noble's short film about a young girl, a stranger to Wainscott, who rescues a child (played by Doug Benedict) from drowning in Georgica Pond. It was the starting point for a nightly walk by adults, children and dogs to Wainscott Cemetery, where grownups honored dead relatives and kids played a ghostly game of hide-

and-seek. Pestered by his kids to install a pool, Charlie Benedict would stand on Kilkare's balcony, point to the Atlantic, and ask: "Why would you want a pool when you have the second biggest pool in the world?"

Now you may understand why I felt I was a Georgica resident when I was really a guest, an insider when I was really an outsider. Simply put, I felt settled in a settlement where people seemed less interested in wealth than wealth of spirit.

Nevertheless, my family's stay in Georgica was brief. In 1970 we left the association for the Bridgehampton Tennis and Surf Club, where the only requirements for admission were a driver's license and a credit card. While my parents enjoyed Georgica's old-fashioned ways, they thought their children deserved a greater number of better amenities: pools, cabanas, a clubhouse with an ocean deck.

I kept roaming Georgica, only this time in the fall and spring as a freelancer of fun. I continued to think I owned the place as I biked the prairie sea and sailed over the speed bumps. Trust me, there's nothing like a Mexican road sign to make a good kid feel like a bad ass.

# Haunts

Proprietor Chauncey Osborn at the Wainscott General Store, where you
could buy everything from penny candy to boat caulk. *(Photo courtesy of
Barbara Wilson D'Andrea and Dennis D'Andrea)*

# THE CEMETERY

The Wainscott Wildcats are practicing a few boys short, which means I'm playing third base-shortstop and left-center. That's a hell of a lot of territory to cover, even on a rectangular field only 38 steps wide. The turf becomes as big as the sea when Pete Dankowski, whose family owns the potato farm behind the backstop, hits a ball over my head that rolls into the cemetery, which doubles as an eternal grandstand.

I hop the metal bars of the cemetery fence to chase the ball, which slams a headstone and shoots toward the one-room school. I chase the ball down, throw it to the cutoff man, look down at a grave, and stop dead in my tracks. By my feet is the final resting place of Gilbert C. Osborn, buried directly across the street from his old general store, where he liked to crack graveyard jokes.

The rest of the game I can't stop thinking about Chauncey Osborn monitoring his beloved business from the great beyond. It's a heavy thought for an 11-year-old. Then again, in the summer of 1969 I had a lot of heavy thoughts about death. That spring my maternal grandmother became my first loved one to pass over. Mary Lardner was a truly beautiful soul, a caregiver by vocation and avocation, an Irish-English nurse who sent me pound notes to buy toy cars and ran her suburban London home as a free lodge. Her death at 69 from lung cancer stunned me and wrecked my mother. I tried to soothe Mom by dedicating a Little League game to Grandma the day she died. I remember more about the dedication than the game, which became fuzzy after I was knocked out by a fastball to the face.

Located by a school, the cemetery schooled me in hard facts. The danger of living by the ocean was illustrated by the grave of

Two views of Wainscott Cemetery, which overlooks one- and two-room schools, a former general store, a potato field, a meadow, a pond and the ocean. *(Photos by Bill Hayward)*

Dayton K. Hedges, who drowned at 19 while sailing without a life preserver. The fickleness of fate was confirmed by the grave of Josiah T. Edwards, who died at 22 when his sloop sank during a storm off the Falkland Islands. Unbelievable epidemics became believable by the graves of victims of the 1918 Flu and the 1865 German Measles.

These lofty reflections became earthy in an extraordinarily ordinary place. The cemetery was only two acres, fairly flat, a square rectangle of soil designated for burying bodies mainly because it was too poor for growing potatoes. The lawn was a motley mix of scorched grass and straggly weeds. A handful of cedar trees were lousy wind breakers. Not a single stone stood out. There were no rugged crosses, no weeping angels, no strikingly geometric shapes. There were only two semi-celebrities among the residents. Charles Heinroth was an organist for Andrew Carnegie, the notorious industrialist. Maginel Wright Enright Barney was a popular illustrator of children's books and a sibling of Frank Lloyd Wright, the notorious architect. Her stone said only that she was "A Creator of Beauty" and Frank's "Little Sis."

Most cemeteries have a holy host of splendid epitaphs. Not Wainscott. The best testimonial was merely tender. Jedediah Osborn, an eighteenth-century soldier killed by an accidentally discharged gun, was memorialized by the simple couplet "How sudden was my death/But fleeting breath." This fond farewell was somewhat sabotaged by the misspelled last name of a memorial patron. Instead of starting over and wiping the slate clean, a lazy, or cheap, mason carved the missing "t" with a caret.

What made the cemetery special was its special location. Even as a kid I understood the lovely logic of burying the dead near so many lively places: a school, a general store, fields of potatoes and wildflowers, a pond, an ocean. Even as a kid I sensed that this plain plot was a magnetic compass for those who wanted to spend the afterlife by their former lives. This cosmic flowchart made more sense as I sat on my bike in the school parking lot, shaded by grand sycamores, and watched visitors treat the cemetery with reverence. They placed flowers by graves, prayed on their knees, cried on their backs. They stared at the sky, held séances in broad daylight, eavesdropped on eternity.

Those pilgrims taught me the morality of mortality. Without asking anyone I learned to walk around the stones, to respect the dead as if they were alive. I refrained from such schoolboy antics as leaving a quarter-full bottle of Boone's Farm Strawberry Hill Wine on Halloween. I never indulged my fantasy of making out at night on a blanket over a grave, settling instead for a roll on a dune.

The cemetery was not only level, it was leveling. It proved that dead farmers are exactly the same as dead lawyers. No matter what their status in life, they share a plan in the hereafter. They want to lie peacefully and gracefully, in a meditation park.

There is room, however, for a little divine intemperance. In the 1840s Thomas and Temperance Hedges were buried under the only stone facing east. Perhaps they wanted a front-row seat at sunrises. Or a head start to East Hampton in foreverland. Or a quicker ticket to Judgment Day Field.

# THE DEAD STORE

In paradise there's always room for improvement. Even though Wainscott was a great playground, I still yearned for a true-blue hangout, a place where all ages and classes could congregate. The post office was too small, the beach too big, the Georgica Association too old, The Forum too young.

The absence of a community center made me intensely interested in a closed community center. There was absolutely nothing lively about the dead general store, which squatted on Wainscott Hollow Road near the cemetery, the one-room school and the rectangular baseball field. The shingled building was a grimy shack, a grim garage with rusty Coca-Cola signs. Yet it drew me like a driftwood tomb.

In time I learned that in the 1930s and '40s the store was a beehive of business and busyness. Here you could buy jugs of kerosene and licorice twirls, Mexican bean beetle insecticide and Old Virginia cigars. You could pick up your mail, have a window installed in your pickup, get your boat caulked. You could discuss pretty much anything—potato prices, hurricanes, war—with pretty much everyone: kids coming from the beach, farmers coming from the fields, wealthy eccentrics coming from other planets.

The store was the hub of David Osborn's world from the time he turned 13. A member of the tenth generation of Osborns born on Main Street, the retired farmer vividly remembers eating blocks of ice cream, baiting rats under the porch with bacon, and drooling over pretty, pretty unattainable girls. In 1946 his calendar queen was Gay Semler, daughter of an attorney who bought 100 acres bordering the Georgica Association and saved the Settlement from encroaching wildfire development. She had blonde hair, blue eyes, wicked curves, a flinty flirtiness—all the essentials of a heart-breaking bombshell.

Miss Semler was tough enough to play touch football on the baseball field opposite the store. Males of all brands lined up to compete against her, hoping for some kind of accidental contact: a tackle, a stiff arm, an illegal hold. "She didn't like anything better than to hang out with a bunch of us horny farmers, from 8 to 80," says Osborn with a laugh. "Everybody in town knew she was the one. Every resort town every summer has a girl like that."

Osborn was also entertained by a pair of rich, nutty sisters who drove to the store in a "quaint" car. Miss Clark was the designated driver and shopper for Mrs. Hitchcock, who never left the vehicle. Sometimes they were accompanied by their brother, who was even nuttier. "He was this crazy old coot," says Osborn, "who would tell us the virtues of collective farming."

One day in the late forties a few locals became a collective of tricksters. After Miss Clark entered the store they jacked up her car an inch. Then they snickered quietly as the auto went nowhere despite her increasingly frantic pedaling to the metal. "Finally, either someone gave the car a friendly push or shoved it off the jack and it went *zooming* down the road," says Osborn. "Of course we were so nonchalant. But, believe me, we were breaking up inside."

The caretaker of this curious circus was proprietor Gilbert C. Osborn, born in 1875 into another branch of Osborns. His middle name was Chauncey; his pet name was "Chancy," a New England contraction. He was perpetually unshaven and wore chronically dirty long johns and overalls. Perhaps he wanted to match the store's filthy décor: sheets of dust; hotel-like holes for rats; flypaper festooned with dead insects. He had a bad limp, courtesy of a hip crushed while moving a house, an injury that ended his career as a boat builder and started his career as a shopkeeper. His pot belly was a sort of store mascot, along with the pot-belly stove. David Osborn blames his girth on too little exercise and too much candy. "Chauncey was accused of eating the profits when no one was around," he says. "He was Santa Claus in the summertime."

Chauncey could be as shifty as a weathervane in the wind. He had very little patience for children who raced every day from school to buy penny candies and yelled with their mouths clotted by licorice whips and caramel pinwheels. The pestering could make him as sour as crabapple fireballs. Scared youngsters swore he was just enough of an ogre to fill his cracker barrel with snapping turtles.

"As a kid you just didn't hang out there," says Norah Pierson, a Georgica Association resident who spent a few months studying in the one-room school. "Chauncey was really intimidating, and so was the store. That place had an unpleasant smell; it took a certain amount of olfactory courage to go in there. The floorboards squeaked and sagged; they were always about to give in under you. I always felt I was in jeopardy of falling through."

Yet Chauncey could be perfectly polite and patient with similarly behaved children. "He was fun and friendly and loved to talk," says Tim Noble, another young resident of the Georgica Association. "He seemed starved for conversation. He'd rather talk than sell."

G. W. Pierson, Norah's father and a Yale history professor, considered Chauncey an entertaining original—a "one-ner" or a "gas man," to quote my Irish relations. Pierson enjoyed hanging out in the general store, listening to Chauncey's "salty, weather-beaten anecdotes," his "fresh-minted sayings," his "hour of speculation about the past." Tim Noble speculates that Chauncey favored Pierson and other Georgica leaders because they were by far his best customers.

Loquacious with insiders, Chauncey could turn taciturn with outsiders. One day a stranger inquired about the whereabouts of Nate Hedges, brother of Chauncey's wife, Mattie, and member of another clan of original Wainscotteers. Chauncey left his stool, waddled over to a shovel, and handed the tool to the visitor. Pointing to the cemetery, he said: "He's across the street."

"Chauncey thought the electricity would be all used up if he spoke too much," says David Osborn with a laugh. "I think he liked to talk about the cemetery because no one would talk back."

The Wainscott General Store in the 1940s, its heyday as business center and social hub. *(Photo courtesy of Barbara Wilson D'Andrea and Dennis D'Andrea)*

Everyone agrees that Chauncey became more social after his wife died in 1944. He immediately increased the store's hours to help relieve his loneliness. Luckily for him, World War II rations created a captive crowd. "You couldn't go anywhere anyway because there was no gasoline," says David Osborn. "Everyone from Georgica would come to the store during the summer after a few weeks with the excuse of buying the evening paper. Back in the forties everybody knew everybody else. We may not have liked them, but we knew them."

Everyone agrees, too, that Chauncey was phenomenally lazy. He kept carrots in a glass jar until they became shriveled roots. He used the same knife to cut ice cream and bacon. His idea of disinfectant was wiping the knife on his pants, which were often stained with kerosene. He typically sat on his stool while customers served themselves loaves of bread, sodas and canned vegetables so old, says Noble, they "came over on the Mayflower." When someone bought a tin of ancient-mariner peas, Chauncey roused himself to dust the top—with his breath.

Chauncey was, in short, a refugee from one of Norman Rockwell's charmingly cranky paintings. He became a national piece of Americana in the forties when Rockwell's primary employer, *The Saturday Evening Post*, ran a "Keeping Posted" profile with a photo of him leaning against the store's gas pump. The story also featured George Hughes, a popular *Post* cover artist who summered in Wainscott and painted a portrait of Chauncey—purpose and whereabouts unknown. David Osborn insists that in the summer of 1946 Hughes and Chauncey vied for Gay Semler's affections, pushing each other to see who could linger with her longer, "until the bitter end."

Perhaps the best sign of Chauncey's status surfaced at the end of summer. Returning to their permanent homes in city or suburb, many of his regular customers stopped by the store to say goodbye until next year. Chauncey liked to point to the cemetery and reply: "Well, I don't know whether I'll be here, or over there."

In 1950 Chauncey moved over there for good, dying in a hospital after he closed the store early one day because he felt sick. At the ripe age of 75 he joined Mattie and their infant daughter Ruth Norris (1912–1912) in a plot directly in line with the shop, where

Ad for Jedi's drive-in on the Montauk Highway in Wainscott, the author's first true-blue hangout. *(Photo by Theo Anderson)*

he could keep tabs on his former life forever. After his death an auctioneer sold most of the store's contents, even nails. In the late fifties the shop was reopened by Chauncey's daughter, Carrie Mae D'Andrea, whose college education and flying lessons were financed by Chauncey's sales of penny candy and boat caulk, and her husband Pasquale, a Navy vet known as Pat. They closed the store for good in the mid-sixties, before my family arrived in town. By then it had a patina of melancholy as gray as its shingles. "I tell you when Chauncey died," says David Osborn, "half the social life in Wainscott died."

In 1968 I got a halfway hangout when Jedi's, a fast-food restaurant, opened in Wainscott on the Montauk Highway. Named for the nickname of a co-owner's son, my future eighth-grade classmate, it served corned-beef sandwiches, egg creams and other New York Jewish deli specialties. While the food and the teen gossip were tasty, the place was too clean, too crammed with tourists. It only made me wish harder that I had been a regular at the dead general store when it was alive, even though I knew that some driftwood is just destined to drift.

# THE SWEET SPOT

My parents' best babysitter was the Penny Candy Shop in Water Mill, also known as the Peace Center of the Hamptons. All they had to do to pacify their bored, bickering kids on long and short drives was merely promise a pit stop at the South Fork's sweetest store. They knew they could buy our cooperation for two quarter bags of licorice shoelaces, Necco wafers and orange-colored, banana-flavored circus peanuts.

Any troubles Meg and I had just seemed to vanish in that circus for the senses. We were seduced by necklaces of pastel-colored rings and coconut-watermelon slices dyed a gloriously gaudy green and pink. We were distracted by jawbreakers that stretched facial muscles and atomic fireballs that burned mouth and brain. Wearing wax lips made us vaudevillians; waving chalky cigarettes made us pint-sized grownups.

Harvey and June Morris, the shop's owners, had the gift of making kids feel like adults and adults like kids. They were gently funny, easily amused and eternally patient, traits that somehow slowed the wicked sugar rush of too many Hershey kisses or chunks of vanilla fudge. They were natural psychologists, sneaky sociologists, not-so-sneaky etiquette teachers, emergency chauffeurs, surrogate parents, capital-C citizens, dream weavers. Their store was the East End's most consistently miraculous place, where every day was Christmas, Easter, Halloween and your birthday.

One of the reasons I wrote this book was to really get to know the people who made my childhood special. I began to learn why the Morrises were special when I interviewed June on the front porch of her tidy rancher in Water Mill, less than a mile from the shop. She was dressed simply yet elegantly, the way I remember her behind the counter. She wore a black shirt, a lime-green jacket and pearls; she could have been a retired librarian. Her distinctive hair—bangs in front, curls in back, "an era all its own"—has been styled by the same woman since 1961, the year she and Harvey became candy merchants.

June and Harvey became shopkeepers by accidental design. Harvey (born in 1924) and June (born in 1927) grew up "up island" in Patchogue, N.Y., where he mowed his family's lawn when it really didn't need mowing, just so he could watch her walk to the bus stop. "His mother used to say: 'We have the best-mowed lawn in the neighborhood—thanks to you,'" says June with a laugh. After they married in 1948, she worked for Brookhaven National Laboratory and he repaired lines and monitored problems for a telephone company. They moved to Water Mill to shorten Harvey's commute to his office in Hampton Bays and lengthen his time fishing on the South Fork, a surf caster's paradise. At the suggestion of his mother, they decided to open a store for crayons, coloring books and other basics for kids like Harvey Morris III, then seven years old. They decided to sell sweets because June had fond childhood memories of visiting a penny-candy store in Patchogue.

The Morrises opened for business on September 11, 1961 in a former shop for children's clothes and haircuts. They weren't entirely ready; the first day they couldn't afford to buy newspapers and cigarettes. Their commercial compass, however, pointed in the right direction right from the start. Their store was located

The Penny Candy Shop in Water Mill was the spot for sweets and acts of sweet citizenship. *(Vintage postcard)*

on the Montauk Highway, the East End's main drag, next to a liquor store, a beacon for summerites and year-rounders alike. The Morrises made their enterprise a beacon, too. For 30 years it was open from 6 a.m. to 9 p.m. seven days a week for most of the year. They sold newspapers to potato farmers who needed to know the prices of their stock before 8 a.m. They sold candy bars to emergency workers during hurricanes. They could afford to stay open when most storekeepers stayed home because for 30 years they lived behind their shop.

From the start the Morris' store doubled as a town hall. Behind the two picture windows and the red awning inscribed "Memories of the Past," you could chew nougats made in France while talking politics, and lick coconut ice cream made in Pennsylvania Dutch

Pennsylvania while reading ads for apartment rentals. "I even sold a house and I wasn't an agent," says June. "One day someone came in and gave me a couple thousand dollars in cash. I looked at the money and I thought: Well, I guess I won't have to work this month."

From the start the store tripled as an entertainment emporium. Visitors were treated to the Morrises' Boxers, all named Chatter; spinning wheels in a window, part of June's collection of antiques, and an assortment of quaint, quirky machines. The candy scale once weighed nails at a hardware store; the century-old cash register could only add up to $3.

The Morrises were treated to the creative rituals of candy addicts. It was Whitley Kaufman's brilliant idea, for example, to minimize the monotony of the 100-mile trip from Wainscott to Manhattan by having his mother give a candy to each of her three boys every 10 miles. Any kid will tell you that sucking on, say, a root-beer barrel sure beats singing, say, "99 Bottles of Beer on the Wall."

I was obsessed by visceral thrills. I loved ripping a Pixie Stick, coating my throat with that tart powder, shaking my head to shake off that mad dash of puckering power. I loved pulling candy buttons from sheets of paper with my teeth, deliciously destroying the symmetry of all those perfect pastel rows. Deciding what to pick—nonpareils? wax juice bottles? bubble-gum cigarettes?—reduced my brain to a sticky jumble, a cerebral caramel pinwheel. I never picked flying saucers, which to me tasted like dissolving paper and gave communion wafers a good name.

June smiled at kids who bit the tops off wax juice bottles and guzzled the fairly tasteless colored water. She laughed at kids who blew the powder off bubble-gum cigarettes to simulate real smoking. She frowned at adults who insisted she was encouraging kids to smoke for real. The only thing she was encouraging, she insisted, was harmless acting.

"You never rushed the kids. I let them take all day making up their mind," says June with a slightly chewy, lightly sticky Patchogue accent. "Sometimes the parents would drive us crazy because they wouldn't let the kids get what they wanted—'Oh no—you don't want *that*.' That wasn't the purpose of the store. If you don't want kids to buy candy, well, leave them at home."

At times the store became a behavioral lab. When adults barged in line in front of children, Harvey set them straight in a hurry. "They wouldn't do it a second time," says June, "I'll tell you that." June watched parents parked outside, waiting to pick up their kids from school, dipping into their youngsters' candy bags and eating their own favorite treats. She must have felt like Willy Wonka, who uses his fantastic chocolate factory to test gratification, greed and generosity.

The Morrises were exceptionally generous inside and outside their shop. Kindergarteners waiting for rides heard June's stories about the store's mascot, a 6-foot-high Paddington Bear. She raised money for the Water Mill Community Club by selling hot dogs at auctions attended by my parents. Harvey, who continued working as a telephone troubleshooter until 1986, raised the hamlet's American flag at sunrise and lowered it at sunset, once leaving a cocktail party early to fulfill his patriotic duty. Both Morrises consoled bus passengers who exited too early, thinking the windmill in Water Mill was really the windmill in East Hampton, their destination. June can't count the number of misguided city people Harvey ferried in his jeep to East Hampton after the night's last bus.

June taught life skills to the girls she hired to work the counter. They wore blouses and skirts because Mrs. Morris thought "dungarees" were undignified. They toted sales on paper bags to limber up their math and keep their accounting honest—"so you could check their addition at the end of the day." June's toughest task was getting her young ladies to treat all the customers, even the rude ones, politely. "I had a hard time getting them to say 'Good morning,' 'Thank you' and 'Have a nice day,'" she says. "I told them they had to say it whether they liked it or not, whether someone spent a hundred dollars or a nickel."

June names a half-dozen former students of her candy charm school. One of the honors graduates is Barbara Wilson, who began working for the Morrises at 12, overcame chronic tardiness and became a judge for the Village and Town of Southampton. June considers Barbara the daughter she never had; Barbara considers June her second mother.

Fifteen minutes after June begins talking about Barbara, Barbara and her real daughter pay June a surprise visit. Fifteen minutes later, an interview becomes a retrospective. June and Barbara recall such loyal locals as Sister Fernanda, who bought bags of sweets for her music students at Villa Maria, a Dominican convent in Water Mill and another June charity. Actor-driver Paul Newman made pit stops after races at the Bridgehampton Race Circuit. Comedian Gilda Radner biked from her Water Mill rental to get her gumball fix. She endeared herself to Barbara by asking pleasantly: "Would you mind fishing for a certain color?"

Both customers and workers were tagged with nicknames. "Mr. Fish" bought more than 100 gummy fish at a time. "The

Jellybean Kid" filled and missed jars, scattering jellybeans that went undetected until spring cleanings. The Morrises were Mr. and Mrs. Penny.

"I tell you, my life has been built around children," says June. "There are no two ways about it." Barbara smiles and adds: "I say God gave Mrs. Morris only one child, so she could take care of everyone else's children."

A happy place turned sad on September 11, 2001. That day the Morrises planned to celebrate their 40th anniversary as candy merchants by closing the store early and dining in Montauk. They canceled their plans after four airplanes hijacked by Muslim terrorists crashed in three states, killing nearly 3,000. "Boy," says June, "we didn't do anything that day."

June suffered another shock in July 2002 when Harvey died from emphysema. His passing transformed the shop into Water Mill's ground zero. The front door was covered with sympathy cards, letters and notes scrawled on paper bags. The post office provided a book for Harvey testimonials.

One day a patron entered the store and laid on the counter an unusual tribute. The scrapbook was filled with clippings from the front pages of newspapers the Morrises saved and customized for the customer. Each banner had the patron's name, written by Harvey, and a decal, applied by June, marking a red-letter day— Independence, St. Patrick's, Valentine's.

June was touched that the regular was touched by her and Harvey's special touches. "I was so overwhelmed—you can't believe how I felt," she says. After a long pause she continues: "You know, at least two or three times a week somebody tells me how much fun they had in our store. We never paid it any mind because we enjoyed it. To us it wasn't really working. I know it sounds crazy but it didn't feel like we were putting our life there—even though we were putting our life there."

# Car Culture

Jim Hall crests in a Chaparral 2G Chevrolet during the 1968 Can-Am at the Bridgehampton Race Circuit, which had dunes and a glorious view of Peconic Bay. *(Photo by Pete Lyons/www.petelyons.com)*

# THE DRIVE-IN

I'm lying under a blanket in the backseat of our 1964 Chevy Impala, snoring through "2001: A Space Odyssey," a blisteringly boring film for an 11-year-old who hates science fiction. Sleeping is my only escape from an incomprehensible, insufferable cast of actors dressed as prehistoric apes screaming at an anachronistic monolith, astronauts babbling about a mission to the moon and a droning, lullabying computer with a superiority complex.

I'm jolted awake by a racket rattling the loudspeaker wedged into the driver's side window. The screeching comes from a space pod rocketing beyond infinity, the only exciting scene in a movie that *Mad*, my favorite funny magazine, dubbed "2001: A Space Idiocy." Drowsiness becomes disorientation as stars explode, colored lights erupt, space haywires and my brain bobsleds through a psychedelic Times Square plugged into Jimi Hendrix's amplifier.

This virtual acid trip happened at the Hamptons Drive-In in Bridgehampton, which was a gas even when the movie sucked. The fun usually began in cars and trucks lined up at the entrance. Being a pretty obedient child, I was amused and amazed by kids hiding under blankets in backseats and pickup beds, laughing loudly because they knew they'd get in for free. They usually succeeded because the cashiers accepted petty crime as normal juvenile hijinks. The guardians at the gate expected to get ripped off just like motorists at a safari park expected baboons to rip off chunks of vinyl roofs.

Once inside the lot, the first order of business was finding a speaker that worked right. It seemed that every third one was disabled—perhaps by the clammy chill of South Fork nights, probably by frustrated customers jamming the contraption between window and door. My father was famously impatient and hunting for a sufficiently loud, clear speaker turned him into the kind of petulant patriarch found in so many of Jean Shepherd's shaggy yarns.

Once hooked up, the next order of business was racing to the playground swings. Yanking my body as hard and as high as I could, trying to touch the dusky sky with my toes, was delightfully liberating and downright magical. It might have been less magical had I known that the kid's stuff at Bridgehampton was, well, kid's stuff. Other drive-ins, I discovered decades later, had pony rides, go-cart tracks and John Wayne promoting "True Grit" by shooting guns on top of a concession stand.

The Bridgehampton concession stand was the site of a memorable rite of passage. In that cinderblock bunker I bought snacks by myself for the first time, rewarding my parents' faith I would return to them safe and with their change. For me, adulthood started the night I purchased a box of Raisinettes and an Orange Crush without adult supervision. Waiting on line I entertained myself by imagining the stand attacked by aliens attracted by the garish fluorescent lights that gave everyone an alien glow.

Back at the car, I engaged in another act of independence. If the night was fairly warm and the crowd was fairly small, my parents let me watch part of the film in a folding chair or, better yet, in the middle of the hood. I didn't care that, separated from speaker and heater, the sound clattered and my teeth chattered. I just loved staring at the screen and the stars, tuning in natural and artificial frequencies, bathing in freedom.

Any ex-teen will tell you that a drive-in is all about freedom. Like any drive-in, Bridgehampton was a cheap, reliable outdoor motel for youngsters in lust and on the lam. Being a junior voyeur, I enjoyed spying on the groping and grinding. One night I returned from the concession stand and followed the sound of moaning to my first vicarious blowjob. When I gasped, the fellated fellow opened his eyes and shot me a look that could have blasted asteroids as if they were hemorrhoids. Luckily for me, I was in the driver's seat. He had to shut up because shouting would have distracted his lady, attracted the flashlight detectives, and blown his ecstasy big time.

There's a saying among Woodstockers that if you remember all the musicians who played the three-day festival, you either weren't there or you didn't drop enough acid. The drive-in spawned a similar saying: If you remember all the films, you either weren't in the passion pit or you didn't get enough passion. Since I wasn't old enough to get enough, I can honestly, accurately say that many Bridgehampton teens spent so much time fooling around in the car, they missed a lot of fooling around on the screen.

Like so many drive-ins in the late sixties and early seventies, Bridgehampton showed plenty of skin. On one hand, the drive-in's owners wanted to cash in on the free-love boom. On the other hand, they needed to compete against racier fare on cable television, a threat they addressed with signs proclaiming "Save Free T.V." Perhaps that's why cashiers let pre-adolescents like me see "The Graduate," where a middle-aged, restless woman commits adultery with a restless, rootless young bachelor, and "Easy Rider," where bikers use peyote as an aphrodisiac.

My parents were agents of corruption, too. They took their kids to R-rated films because they knew we'd be bored to sleep, which would give them a relatively rare night out and still maintain family unity. That's why "2001," which was originally released in 1968, was my surreal sleeping pill and hallucinogenic alarm clock in the summer of 1969, when it was re-released to feed the frenzy over the Apollo 11 moon landing. That's why I saw "I Love You, Alice B. Toklas," a sex comedy about a bored middle-aged lawyer who clicks with a hippie chick who bakes hash brownies—and who gave my proper, scone-baking English mother a burning desire to make chocolate pot.

The Hamptons Drive-In in Bridgehampton, site of so many weirdly wonderful double features. *(Photo by Steve Singer / Courtesy of Paul Brennan)*

Ad for "2001: A Space Odyssey," a 1968 release re-released at the drive-in in 1969 to coincide with the Apollo 11 moon landing. *(Photo by Theo Anderson)*

Against all odds the drive-in made me a film fan. Despite being bored and cold and distracted and drowsy, I became an aficionado of all sorts of actors, genres and formats. At Bridgehampton I saw "You Only Live Twice," which made me admire Sean Connery's suave, witty James Bond; the 007 satire "Casino Royale," which made me admire Woody Allen's clownish kvetching, and "To Sir, with Love," which made me admire Sidney Poitier's radiant, raging dignity. At Bridgehampton I saw my first horror movie: "The Sand Pebbles," a drama about a U.S. Navy gunboat patrolling 1920s China. For a good week I had nightmares about a hot-headed machinist, played by Steve McQueen, who shoots to death a coolie tortured onshore by nationalists, axes a nationalist after he helps break a blockade of junks, and is shot to death by a sniper in a deserted, haunted palace. The violence, so foreign and yet so personal, scared me into thinking I'd be drafted and become the first American sub-teen to die during hand-to-hand combat in Vietnam.

Bridgehampton birthed my bizarre fondness for pastel-colored, flawless-skinned, perfectly fizzy pictures like "Sweet November" and "Those Magnificent Men in Their Flying Machines." Bridgehampton can be blamed for my love affair with daffy, only-at-the-drive-in double bills like "If It's Tuesday, It Must Be Belgium," a comedy about tourists breaking down, and "Let It Be," a documentary about the Beatles breaking up. The only connection between those films is that both take place in Europe. That, and the fact that so many people in a summer resort are so bored at night they'll watch pretty much any kind of crap.

Best of all, Bridgehampton encouraged me to dig movies so bad they're good. Five decades later, "2001" still makes me yawn, still makes me want to scream like an ape, still gives me a good psychotropic jolt. The only thing better would be my mother finally baking me a batch of Alice B. Toklas-toked brownies.

Hmmmm. Maybe the only way to really, truly enjoy "2001" is stoned.

# AUSTIE

One of the landmarks on the Montauk Highway in Southampton was a big blue building that imitated an airplane hanger with three humps. Behind that bulky steel façade was every conceivable classic car: primitive, elegant, sporty, crazy, exotic, erotic, extinct. Inside that cavernous garage my heart burned rubber and my imagination popped a wheelie.

One of my favorite vintage vehicles was the 1907 Thomas Flyer that won a 1908 around-the-world race from Times Square to Paris. I couldn't believe that such a basic automobile—basically, an open-air wagon with a steering wheel and a motor—traveled nearly 22,000 miles over 169 days. Another top choice was a Pierce Silver Arrow made for the 1933–1934 Century of Progress International Exposition in Chicago. I was less impressed by the pedigree than the sleek, smart body. The recessed door handles, the tapered back, the front fenders that stored spare wheels—here was my first piece of moving sculpture.

The adventure continued around the grounds. For no trip to the Long Island Automotive Museum was complete without cruising a backyard dirt road in an antique hook-and-ladder fire engine that spewed smoke and lurched like a cranky freight train. Cranking the ear-slapping, window-rattling siren made me feel like the captain of the resident Sandy Hollow Fire Company.

The museum was, in short, a candy store. Somehow it makes sense it was owned and operated by an heir to the Jack Frost sugar empire, a man with a sweet tooth for classic cars. Raised in Flushing, Queens, Henry Austin "Austie" Clark Jr. was a Harvard freshman when he acquired his first early auto, a Ford Model T made in 1915, two years before he was born. After leaving the

Automotive impresario Henry Austin "Austie" Clark Jr. lets actor Gary Cooper, his friend and fellow classic-car collector, take the wheel of Clark's Simplex speedster. *(Photo courtesy of Walter McCarthy)*

Navy, where he served as a radar technician in World War II, he began collecting vintage vehicles in earnest. By 1948 he owned 35, some of which he exhibited in his new Southampton museum in a three-bay Quonset hut.

Clark was a detective with flair. He found that 1933 Pierce Silver Arrow, for example, in a junkyard in Cicero, Ill. He bought it because it was stylish, because it was one of only six made that year, and because he could easily polish its provenance. The holes in the trunk, he loved to say, were made by bullets fired by gangsters employed by Al Capone, the car's original owner and Public Enemy No. 1.

Clark doubled as a canny archaeologist and an uncanny psychologist. "My father amassed his collection in large part because widows wanted these hulks hauled out of their garages," says his son, Henry Austin "Hal" Clark III. "He had all sorts of stuff, from the ridiculous to the sublime. He had 17 cars that no one knew existed."

In his heyday Clark owned some 250 autos and countless other motorized devices (i.e., a gas-powered pogo stick). What separated him from other collectors was his role as a one-stop shop. His museum hosted "The Iron Range," a sporadic flea market of rare parts, many made of brass from the 1890s to World War I, a period dubbed "The Brass Era." His house in Glen Cove, Long Island, was a museum of rare books and catalogs, photographs and postcards, paintings and trophies. Visitors could read car magazines owned by Kaiser Wilhelm in a pair of bucket seats from a Locomobile, made by the maker of an early internal combustion engine. Today, they can see most of Clark's archives at the Henry Ford Museum in Dearborn, Mich., a first-rate repository of Americana created by the visionary behind Clark's first classic car.

Clark filtered his encyclopedic knowledge into *The Standard Catalog of American Cars, 1802–1945*, a bible for collectors and historians. He was the chief researcher for writer and good friend Beverly Rae Kimes, an acclaimed auto authority who shared his fondness for driving the corkscrew turns between fact, fiction and fable. He strained his love of interviewing, editorializing and yarning into "Young Nuts and Old Bolts," a 1972–1978 column in *Old Cars* magazine (now *Old Cars Weekly*). A preservationist to his chassis, he even bought the rights to a dead company, Simplex, which customized luxury autos for the Rockefellers.

Clark's many lives were shared by Dave Brownell, founding editor of *Old Cars*, former editor of *Hemmings Motor News* and boon companion. Brownell edited Clark's columns, traded information with Clark on auctions and appraisals, raced Clark's cars. He even bought one of Clark's cars, a 1924 Bentley 3 Litre. In a pair of interviews from his Vermont home, he recalls Austie as a 120-mph rogue.

I met Austie in 1967 in Manhattan at an auction of vintage auto memorabilia. All he did was basically outbid me on every piece. Afterward I said to him: "You're Henry Austin Clark."

"The one and the same."

"I was chasing a number of the things you bought."

"Oh, are you are automotive art collector?"

"A budding collector."

"Oh, you must come back to the house and I'll show you some things you probably haven't seen."

So I went out to Glen Cove and spent a delightful afternoon with him. I bought a couple of pieces at very, very reasonable prices. I was charmed by an early French print of a guy behind the wheel of a car, wearing a checkered hat, with a lady. They're flying along in the breeze and she has a big Gibson Girl hat on, with a bow strung around her chin. I thought it was a very, very nice embodiment of what early motoring was about. There was also a poster of a Zust [made in 1905–1917], one of the participants in that New York to Paris race in 1908. It was done by a famous German Expressionist artist. A very arresting piece.

I remember there was this great painting in his library: J. C. Leyendecker's "Mercedes at Madison Square." A classic piece: it was on the cover of the 1905 *Collier's* automobile supplement. I vowed to myself: I'm gonna have that. I did eventually get it. I used to look at it every night. I'd study Leyendecker's brush work, just the way he'd do a brass lamp with one twist of color.

That's how our friendship began. It was worth losing out to him.

Another time we were going into the city to an auction of auto memorabilia from the estate of [auto journalist] Ken Purdy. Ken was a guy who interested a lot of people in old cars and car collecting with his enthusiasm. He had a very romantic way of talking; one of his books was called *Kings of the Road*. Austie's wife Waleta—"Wally"—could be tough; he nicknamed her "The War Department." Before we went to the auction she told Austie: "You've got enough stuff here; don't you dare bring anything home." And he said: "Yes, dear"—which was always his response to her.

Austie was an inveterate collector. So of course we loaded that car with so much stuff, it was dragging. After we stopped at every topless place on Queens Boulevard—he was a collector of pulchritude, too—we came back to Glen Cove at midnight and hid stuff in the cellar, so Wally wouldn't see it right away.

The next morning Wally asks Austie: "What did you buy at auction?" "Nothing," he says. And she says: "Well, you must have bought something, because there's something wrong with the rear springs."

Austie used to hold these gatherings in the backyard of his house in Glen Cove. It was a wonderful microcosm of terrific automobiles and terrific people. I remember one time they had to go out and rescue Charles Addams [cartoonist, vintage car collector and Clark friend] because his Bugatti had crapped out on the Long Island Expressway.

So they brought it back to Glen Cove and somebody started fiddling with it. And "Gggggaaaa!" Somebody said, "Wait a minute," and stuck his hand in the carburetor and pulled out an honest-to-God butterfly. It was blocking the air intake. He started it again and this time it turned over: "Gggggaaaa—vrrroom!" And I said to myself: "Only a Bugatti could be stopped by a butterfly."

The Thomas Flyer—that was the crown jewel in Austie's collection, in a way. Yet he could never get George Schuster to actually verify that was the car that he drove when he won the around-the-world race in 1908. That was one of the great collecting frustrations of Austie's life.

I'd say my favorite vehicle of his was his [1911] Mercer [Type 35] Raceabout. It was designed by Finley [Robertson] Porter, a Long Islander who said he wanted to make great cars for the public. It's probably one of the great genius designs of the early twentieth century. The steering is pinpoint accurate. The balance of those cars, the performance—they were the Corvettes of their time. It's one of my dream cars.

Austie was always a grand host. One year he hosted the Pioneer Automobile Touring Club for Brass Era cars. I didn't have a Brass Era car so he lent me his Mercer for five days. We were doing demo laps at the [Bridgehampton] Race Circuit and I was trying to be very careful and take care of Austie's car and this guy [Bill Campbell] in a [1910] Stevens Duryea—a great lumbering car— chops me on the corner. Well, that got my dander up and I went by that Stevens Duryea like it was tied to a post. And I looked at the sweep hand on the speedometer and it was 94 mph—the highest speed in any segment.

Well, I told Austie I was a bad boy. And Austie looked at the speedometer and he smiled and he said: "You weren't a bad boy.

You were a good boy." Anybody else would have torn their hair out. His attitude was: Did you enjoy the car? And, boy, did I ever!

He loved his Model T fire chief's car. He loved fire engines—probably as much as cars. He had this bright idea he wanted his own fire department, so he started the Sandy Hollow Fire Company. He appointed his friends as captains with badges. I was disappointed that I never became an honorary captain. I'd pester him but he never gave one to me. I know plenty of people who dodged speeding tickets because they had that badge. The badges—and Austie's good relations with the local authorities—saved their bacon.

One time Austie wrote the outfit that made police and fire department badges and asked for maybe 40 captain's badges. I guess somebody at the company called up and said: "Excuse me, the only time we've gotten a request like this was from New York City." And Austie said: "Don't worry about it—my credit's good."

Austie was always holding these sales of old parts, rusty parts, bits for cars at the museum. They were called the Iron Range or Early Iron and they went back to the fifties. It was never a formal announcement; you just sort of found out through the old-car telegraph. There were a lot of old, decrepit chassis—a bunch of skeletons of early cars—hanging around the back of the museum. If they weren't so old, it would simply be a junkyard.

The last Iron Range I went to, Austie had a radiator shield from an SS Jaguar just sitting in the corner. "Austie," I said, "how much is the SS Jaguar?"

"That's not a Jaguar, that's a '32 Chrysler."

"No," I said, "that's an SS Jaguar."

"Don't argue with Uncle Austie."

"Alright, how much is the '32 Chrysler?"

So I bought it—and sold it to a Jag guy.

At some point he'd halt all the business at the Iron Range and announce it was time for lunch. We'd pile on the old Autocar bus and ride to Herb McCarthy's [a favorite Clark restaurant-watering hole in Southampton]. Going down was okay; coming back was a little bit interesting because we had done a bit of drinking. Let me tell you, that thing wasn't easy to drive when you were dead sober.

If you were smart, you waited Austie out on the Iron Range. People in the know knew that after a few drinks at McCarthy's, by the time he got back to the Iron Range he was a lot easier to deal with on the price.

It's a privilege to know some people, and that's the way I felt about Austie. I mean, the depth of his knowledge was awe inspiring. He had a steel-trap mind when it came to finding stuff and minutiae. And the resources he had in that library were just mind boggling. Well, he couldn't have had a *Standard Catalog* without it; that book did more for the history of the American auto than anything else. And he was never one of these guys to throw his weight around. If you made a mistake, he wouldn't jump all over you. He knew better than most people, and he was content to know.

There was no pretense about him. Here he is, the son of wealth, living in the private enclave of Glen Cove, has a summer home in Southampton—he could have been a hideous snob. Instead, he was one of the great guys. Believe me, there are an awful lot of cars that wouldn't be on the road if it wasn't for his parts. He just wanted to see those cars get back on the road. And he was so generous. He had all this literature, all this ephemera, and he donated the whole shooting match to the Henry Ford Museum. In his own quiet way he had a real mission for the preservation of automotive history. That was his work; that was his job. I think he always enjoyed what he was doing. He enjoyed it so much; he wanted everybody else to enjoy it too. And there's nothing wrong with that.

I learned so much from him. One time he told me: "You know and I know these early cars don't start a damn. So lesson number one, when you're guiding one of these cars, is try to keep it rolling. Don't stop unless you absolutely have to." Because it's much more difficult to go through the gears than it is to keep the car rolling.

Austie proved his point in a [1906] Pungs-Finch [Limited, the first automobile with a hemi-powered engine]. It was a very powerful early car; I think he had the only surviving one. He was going into Southampton to fill it up with gas. And my wife was invited to ride along with him. So off he went and they got to the first traffic light and he hit the brake pedal and there was nothing there. So he kind of held the steering wheel and stood up and surveyed the situation and said: "Out of the way—I have no brakes!" And hoped that people could hear him.

The other thing he taught me is you shouldn't take yourself too seriously. Life should have some fun to it. When Austie died, my ex-wife had a very trenchant observation. "You know," she said, "his entire life was one long fraternity party." That about sums him up. If you liked cars and you liked an occasional drink and you liked to have a good time, you were his guy.

I remember one time we were on the Glidden Tour [for Brass Era cars], staying at the Lake Placid Hotel; I remember I was using

Austie's Mercer. And Wally told Austie: "Our neighbor [in Glen Cove] just lost the presidency of the Chase Manhattan Bank." And Austie says: "It serves the son of a bitch right—he could never make a decent martini."

I just about fell on the floor. That's just about pure W. C. Fields; that's such pure Austin Clark.

# THE BRIDGE

I'm standing on the Chevron pedestrian bridge at the Bridgehampton Race Circuit, watching heaven duel hell. It's the 1967 Chevron Grand Prix Can-Am, and some of the world's fastest drivers are challenging one of the world's nastiest tracks. Dan Gurney, Jim Hall and 28 others squeezed into fiberglass spaceships with big wheels and giant fenders are whipping through wicked turns shielded by dunes, jackhammering around a bumpy hairpin, pushing gravity to the metal. Over 110 minutes and 200 miles they turn the course into an obstacle course of sand, stones, smoke, flames, oil and an unhinged door.

I'm unhinged by the thundering noise, zigzagging cars, flashing metallic colors, burning fuel, sizzling heat and blindingly bright light. Even the peaceful horizon, with steeples in Sag Harbor and sailboats on Peconic Bay, is strangely dizzying. The bridge is shaking, but only because I am.

Down in the crowd is a famous actor who knows my queasiness. Paul Newman, a champion racing fan, is in the pits because he's sponsoring Mario Andretti's electric-violet Honker Ford. Watching the crazy ballet of figure eights and fishtails reminds him of his harrowing ride the day before in a pace car driven by Andretti, his first spin with a professional driver as well as his first spin around the Bridgehampton track. The roller coaster in a Shelby Cobra Mustang jarred Newman's vital organs and left him believing that Custer's Last Stand must have been a kiddie ride.

A stock-car driver named David Pearson made a grand declaration about the Bridge before he began practicing there for the 1966 NASCAR grand championship. "This here is the end of the earth," he said, "and that ain't no shit." Well, he was almost right. You see, for a car-crazy kid like me, the Bridge was the end of the earth *and* the shit.

My parents swore my third word was "car," which, because I couldn't cough out a "c," came out as "gar." No one knows why. Maybe I inherited my paternal grandfather's lust for roadsters, an acceptable sin for a mighty Mennonite minister. Maybe I was conceived in the sporty Pontiac my father sold before I was born for a more sensible sedan.

Whatever the reason, by age five I was an auto addict. Using pound notes sent by my English grandmother for birthdays and holidays, I bought metal scale models of the coolest cars made by the coolest companies: Corgi, Matchbox, Dinky. Most of my purchases were curvy and quirky. I owned a Ferrari Berlinetta 250

Driver Mario Andretti talks shop with actor Paul Newman, co-owner of Andretti's fabled Honker Ford, during a practice for the 1967 Can-Am at the Bridgehampton Race Circuit. *(Photo by Chris Economaki / Courtesy of Corinne Economaki)*

Le Mans because of a boss rear engine, a Lotus Elan S2 because of a funky ad on the trunk: "Put a Tiger in Your Tank."

Like most kid collectors, I was mesmerized by moving parts. I spent hours opening the rear-facing doors of a black Rolls-Royce Phantom V, flipping the red bucket seats of a gold Camaro SS. I spent days operating the gadgets on the James Bond Aston-Martin D.B. 5, which I snapped up after seeing the real deal in the movie "Goldfinger." I felt like a spy-in-training ejecting a fingernail-sized villain from the passenger seat, pressing the exhaust pipes to pop a bullet shield.

My love for toy cars came from nowhere. My love for real cars came from the South Fork. Even as an elementary schooler I realized that sexy automobiles became sexier on those flat roads along those sweeping fields washed by that lush light. I had my first vehicular orgasm when a candy-apple-red 1965 Mustang convertible cruised Lamb Avenue in Quogue, where we were renting a house, blasting Bob Dylan's "Like a Rolling Stone." More thrill rides followed: a Karmann Ghia gunning the back roads between Sagaponack and Bridgehampton; an MGB GT dragging the desert-like strip between Amagansett and Napeague; a hemi-powered Barracuda sailing over the slaloming Old Montauk Highway.

I had no idea that some of these roads were racetracks before I was born. From 1949 to 1953 a host of speed demons—many ex-soldiers, some retired fighter pilots—pushed Jaguars, Porsches and other new European roadsters over 130 mph over four-plus miles of pavement in Bridgehampton and Sagaponack. Bold-faced drivers ranged from Dave Garroway, the first host of the "Today" show, to Briggs Cunningham, a legend for his high finishes at the

24 Hours of Le Mans in hybrid cars (i.e., "LeMonstre," a Cadillac coupe with an aerodynamic aluminum body developed by aircraft engineers) and skippering the winning yacht in the 1958 America's Cup. Races were supervised by a consortium of East End speed moguls. Financial pole sitters included Henry Austin "Austie" Clark Jr., whose Long Island Automotive Museum featured such early hot rods as a 1907 Thomas Flyer, and Bruce Stevenson, an energy investment manager and Royal Air Force alumnus who jump-started street racing on the South Fork after a three-decade hibernation.

The Bridgehampton Road Race was scenic and magnetic, annually attracting upwards of 180 drivers and 40,000 spectators. It was also dangerous, with snow fences and hay bales masquerading as safety barriers. In 1953 local governors canceled the popular street competition after three spectators were hit by a car dodging a pedestrian chasing a runaway hat. The same year Clark, Stevenson and service-station owner B. J. "Mummy" Corrigan decided to fill the racing void by building a safer, bolder, out-of-town track. They spent the next three years buying nearly 600 acres of Bridgehampton land chartered in 1685 by King James II. The byzantine operation involved the purchase of hundreds of lots—most used for fishing, hunting and foraging, many with long-lost owners.

The leaders of the fledgling Bridgehampton Road Races Corporation had earthy, lofty plans. They sold stocks for $5 apiece from a card table by the Candy Kitchen, a Bridgehampton luncheonette, ice-cream parlor and social center. They commissioned two Grumman Aircraft engineers to design the track. It ended up being largely developed by the man who bulldozed its roads, contours and hazards: Ercole Colasante, an Italian race car driver and team manager. He was inspired by a jigsaw puzzle of glacial debris and three daring European courses, particularly a Dutch track snaking through trees and dunes.

The Bridge opened in 1957 with races for cars, motorcycles, bicycles and even runners. Shaped like an abstract whale, the course had the bite of a Great White shark. The 2.85 miles of asphalt pavement featured bumpy and sandy patches, four elevation changes totaling 130 feet and eight turns. The first turn, the Millstone, was famously hair- and hell-raising—a true millstone. After hitting up to 170 mph on a 3,100-foot straightaway, drivers had to prepare for three right-hand bends—all quick, all downhill, all blind, all scary. Only a yellow light and a flagman warned racers of breakdowns, crashes and other looming catastrophes.

"You didn't dare miss that first bend," says Mario Andretti. "You had to be very precise. If you didn't know where you were going, you could get lost. You'd end up in Long Island Sound—or Coney Island."

Indeed, the Bridge was a Hamptons version of Coney Island. Drivers registered in a Water Mill restaurant owned by Dick Ridgely, who drummed in a band led by Paul Whiteman, the renowned jazz impresario. Beautiful bun-haired women in sleeveless sheet dresses listened to jazz and sipped cocktails under a tent by the Circuit Club, an exclusive paddock with a picket fence, picnic tables and an antique bar salvaged by Austie Clark, who loved to tend his bar. They hobnobbed with celebrities attracted by first-rate drivers attacking a track with a top-notch reputation as a bitch goddess. Among the A-listers were Vincent Sardi, restaurateur and amateur racer; James Garner, amateur racer, race car owner and star of the television series "Maverick" and the racing film "Grand Prix," and Walter Cronkite, the nation's anchorman.

Some races were prefaced by laps from vintage sports cars. Clark showcased his 1914 Duesenberg-Mason, which was identical to an Indy 500 vehicle driven by Capt. Eddie Rickenbacker, the World War I flying hero. Sometimes Clark was joined by his friend Charles Addams, the gloriously ghoulish cartoonist, Westhampton Beach resident and owner of a 1926 Bugatti T 35 C Grand Prix, manganese blue and very, very sweet. In 1959 Addams raced at the Bridge in a rare 1923 Mercedes built for the Indy 500, the same machine he raced in 1952 on streets in Bridgehampton and Sagaponack.

Spectators at the Bridge read programs with an Addams cover illustration. They sat in stands imported from the Polo Grounds, the demolished home of the New York Giants and New York Mets; camped in infield tents, and moved from site to site in tractor-drawn hay carts. One of the best spots for these "mountain goats" was Arents Corner, which had a lovely view of Peconic Bay and was nearly, thrillingly over the track. Its namesake was George Arents III, who in 1957 tested the unopened course by demolishing a new Ferrari—which he could afford to buy, repair and replace as an American Tobacco Company heir.

I liked cars more for their looks than their guts; lyrical lines meant more to me than horses under the hood. Likewise, I liked drivers at the Bridge less for their success than their story. I really didn't care that Peter Revson failed to finish three races in 1967–1969, that he was victimized by suspension and gearbox problems. What appealed to me was his snappy combination of intelligence and recklessness, Ivy League hipness and movie-star charisma. His sideburns were the best in the business; I wanted to grow a pair like them like I wanted to wear a Nehru jacket. If I had his handsomeness, I figured, I could date the gorgeous girls who flocked and flirted around him. Of course I ignored the fact that Revson, to quote *Sports Illustrated* writer Robert F. Jones, looked "like a $10,000 bill must feel."

To me, Revson seemed exotic because he won grand prixes in Europe. He polished his pedigree by finishing second in the 1970 12 Hours of Sebring with teammate Steve McQueen, who was more of a speed junkie than fellow actors Garner or Newman. Revson grew up privileged, the child of a cofounder of Revlon, the cosmetics giant. Yet he paid his bills and his dues. He kept racing even after his brother Doug, a driving colleague, died in a 1967 crash. His zest for life was inscribed on a pillbox he received from a female fan: "Everything Is Sweetened By Risk."

I liked Mario Andretti because he lived in Nazareth, Pa., near my father's hometown. He was also a bona fide underdog, a species my dad taught me to appreciate. His car career was pure bootstrap. At age five he and his twin brother, Aldo, raced hand-made wooden cars over the hills of their Italian village. In Nazareth, where the brothers Andretti settled at 15, he competed on oval dirt tracks in a rebuilt 1948 Hudson Hornet Sportsman. By 1964 he had conquered every racing class from midget to sprint.

There was something endearing about Andretti's checkered career at the Bridge. It was here, in 1965, that he drove his first sports car, a Ferrari 275P, for the North American Racing Team run by Luigi Chinetti, a fabled ex-driver, mechanic and early Ferrari advocate in the United States. Andretti was at a disadvantage even before he turned on the ignition. "I had never seen the course, so the blind hairpins were doubly blind," he says from his office in

Nazareth, a half hour from my home. "Before the first practice, I didn't even know if the first turn was right or left."

That weekend Andretti wrestled the Bridge to a draw. He was in third place when his Ferrari was retired prematurely by a bad clutch. While the Chinetti team was satisfied with him, he wasn't satisfied with himself. "That day I was not quick enough," he says, "to rub wheels with the big boys." The breakdown was especially disappointing during a breakthrough year when he was named the Indy 500's top rookie and became the youngest United States Auto Club series champion.

In 1967 Andretti returned to the Bridge for the Chevron Grand Prix Can-Am. His car, a Holman-Moody Honker-II Ford 427, was famously unreliable, or "slippery." Despite a respectable eighth-place finish, he insists it's the worst vehicle he ever raced. The race wasn't a total loss; after all, he met Paul Newman for the first time. In fact, he learned the actor was on his team when he saw "Paul Newman" on the Honker's nose. "I think I'll paint my name on it," joked Andretti over the public-address system after a practice, "and let Paul drive it."

That weekend Newman wanted no part of driving the Bridge. He learned his lesson while riding with Andretti in a pace car from hell. When the reconnaissance run was over, Newman ejected himself from "the infernal machine," belly flopped in the pit, "kissed the ground, thanked my Maker, and vowed never to kick my dog."

Despite the unfriendly introduction, Newman quickly befriended the Bridge. Andretti believes the demanding course compelled Newman to become a more devoted racing actor, owner and driver. In 1969 he starred in the film "Winning," playing an obsessed driver who fights a rival for the affections of his long-suffering wife, played by Newman's real-life spouse, Joanne Woodward, who entertained herself at the Bridge by chatting with spectators, some of whom petted her dogs. In 1983 Newman and Carl Haas, an Andretti rival on the Can-Am circuit, formed an Indy team with Andretti as driver. In the eighties Newman regularly raced at the Bridge, becoming a respected competitor. In the eighties and nineties he endorsed a campaign to prevent the course from becoming a condominium complex and golf course.

My main man at the Bridge was Mark Donohue, a main competitor of Andretti and Revson and a driver with Newman-like creativity and intensity. I began following him during that 1967 Can-Am, which he won in a blue, bodacious Lola T70 Mk.3B Chevy. The next year he won the Trans-Am in a Camaro Z28, a souped-up version of one of my favorite sports cars. My admiration grew as I listened to gear heads in the stands celebrate him as that rare driver who could engineer and customize his cars. I was particularly fascinated by the story of Donohue and Roger Penske, his team owner, lightening and quickening the Camaro by dipping its frame in paint-stripping acid. What sounded like vehicular voodoo was what Donohue called "the unfair advantage."

Donohue and the Bridge were true comrades. In 1964 he won his first significant race there, a 500-mile marathon. He drove an MGB owned by his mentor, Walter Hansgen, one of the track's best and best-loved drivers. In 1967–1970 Donohue was the course's most successful competitor, winning four races, two more than the runner-up. During the 1968 Vanderbilt Cup he broke the Bridge speed record, finishing a lap in 91.33 seconds in a McLaren M6A

Cheverolet. By then he had mastered the course's demands of agility and aggression, especially under rainy conditions. He had also conquered a turn named for Hansgen, who died from injuries suffered during a 1966 practice for Le Mans.

A scientist of speed, Donohue made the Bridge his personal laboratory. It was there that he tested the Camaro Z28 on ice at sunset; it was there that, after winning the 1967 Can-Am by default, he decided to shape up. One of the first drivers to embrace situps and healthy foods, he radically improved his alertness, endurance and success. In 1967 he won six of the eight races he entered for the U.S. Road Racing Championship. In 1968 he won a stunning 10 of 13 Trans-Ams and finished seventh in his first Indy 500, receiving rookie of the year honors. In 1972 he won his first Indy in style, setting a speed record of 162 mph.

The 1969 Trans-Am gilded Donohue's mythic status at the Bridge. He won the pole position in a Camaro Z28 with holes poked in doors to cool rear tires and brakes. After killing the motor during a warm-up, he borrowed a Camaro from Penske teammate Ronnie Bucknum and was demoted from the front of the pack to the back for driving an unqualified car. Pissed off by the chief steward's verdict, even though he knew it was right, Donohue started the race a whopping 500 yards behind the pack—"just to make sure there was no confusion."

There was no confusion during the race. After the first lap, Donohue advanced from 30th place to 12th. Despite breaking a pushrod and losing a cylinder, he finished second, 109 seconds behind a Mustang Boss 302 driven by George Follmer, a former and future teammate who that season was Donohue's rough rival, banging fenders and nearly banging heads.

Three years later Donohue accused Follmer of a weird kind of infidelity when the latter tested a Donohue-modified Porsche 917 10K "Turbo Panzer" for the Penske team while Donohue recuperated from an accident. "It just doesn't feel right," wrote Donohue in *The Unfair Advantage*, his memoir-manual. "Seeing another man drive your car, a car you know so well. I imagine it must feel like watching another man in bed with your wife."

It was this gutsy honesty that made me a Donohue fan. He was funny enough to invent a menu featuring bulls' balls, philosophical enough to toast a near-fatal accident by hosting a "Crash & Burn" party, colorful enough to turn fans into fanatics. In fact, Al Holbert, a driver who fixed cars for Sam Posey, another Donohue rival, actually learned to imitate Donohue's handwriting, a rather extreme form of idolatry.

It was Donohue who made the Bridge my bridge to nowhere, the only place where I was seduced by speed, strategy and danger. The track inspired me to run my Hot Wheels off their plastic orange track, play pit crew with my Corgi Ferrari Berlinetta, and gorge on racing films at the Hamptons Drive-In in Bridgehampton. That's where I saw Garner in "Grand Prix," McQueen in "Le Mans" and Newman in "Winning."

Newman stars in one of my favorite tales of the Bridge. One day the actor was approached during a practice by Carl Jensen, the track's superintendent and a weekend projectionist at the drive-in. "You know," Jensen told Newman, "you and I are in the same business."

"You mean racing?" asked Newman.

"No," said Jensen, "the movies."

# Landmarks

Architect Norman Jaffe designed this 1969 avant-garde farmhouse in Wainscott for photographer/filmmaker Harold Becker, later the director of "Taps," "Sea of Love" and other features. *(Photo courtesy of Alastair Gordon)*

# THE SPHINX

In 1969 I got my own personal sphinx. I spent the entire summer, and many seasons thereafter, answering the riddle of why I was mesmerized by a new house seemingly built by masons from outer space.

All that was visible from Town Line Road was a silhouette of stones. The tall wall had a roof that plunged like a ski slope, a gabled tower that topped 30 feet and an absurdly small door made more absurd by the complete absence of windows. The shell was connected to a low wall, a 7-foot-high, over 50-foot-long, mostly stone fence that screened a vast pasture a quarter mile from the ocean. Made of inflexible materials, the structure was remarkably flexible, imitating everything from a modern medieval barn to the back of a huge fireplace.

The place not only took my breath away, it blew me away. It beat the living shit out of every single home I knew on the South Fork. It was immensely more dramatic than the trim shingled saltboxes that dotted shady streets, dramatically smarter than the Rubik's Cube boxes that blighted potato fields. It was sublimely outrageous, a Zen shout.

The house, it turned out, was the vision of two visual visionaries. Harold Becker, the client, directed television commercials and took still photographs for movies. Born in 1932, the New York City native satisfied his creative needs by making short documentaries about radicals: photographer Eugene Atget, the Paris street sociologist; Blind Gary Davis, the blues-gospel guitarist who influenced generations with his finger picking; civil-rights activist Ivanhoe Donaldson, who brought food to

Mississippi sharecroppers evicted for trying to register to vote. Using a restored 11-by-14 view camera from the twenties, Becker photographed naked women as abstractions, focusing on the tiny cracks of a shaved leg or heel calluses. Today, he's best known as the director of such feature films as "Sea of Love" and "City Hall," the latter written by Bo Goldman, who in the late sixties owned a Sagaponack seafood shop where Becker bought lobster salad.

Like Becker, architect Norman Jaffe alternated between commercial and personal projects. Also born in 1932, the Seattle native supported himself in the sixties with bread-and-butter commissions: a Manhattan bachelor pad for Becker; a regional headquarters for an industrial gas company; a cluster of sloping-roofed, light-boxed, linked contemporary cabins. What he really

Norman Jaffe lounges by a model for a romantic-modernist home he designed, looking like a model in a "What Sort of Man Reads Playboy?" ad. *(Photo courtesy of Alastair Gordon)*

yearned to do was create buildings that embraced and extended their settings—true landscape architecture. For a Virginia family he designed but never executed a strikingly geometric home with cascading rectangular balconies, a kind of contemporary cliff dwelling. He was honoring and challenging Fallingwater, a collection of cantilevered slabs hovering over a Pennsylvania waterfall conceived by Frank Lloyd Wright, one of Jaffe's revolutionary role models.

Jaffe found his muse on and in the South Fork, his first architectural siren. Treating the area as a score, he played jazz with the sweeping fields; the painterly, Vermeer-tinged light; the seamless junction of land, sky and sea with "an inexhaustible variation of spirit." In 1968 he finished his first East End residences, all in Bridgehampton, each organic. The Schulman House was another Wrightian hybrid—a recessed, thrusting, rectilinear cruise ship on sandy, grassy waves. He developed two very different homes for composer Alexander "Sascha" Burland, author of the "What's My Line?" theme and vocalist for the Nutty Squirrels, a jazzy rival of the Chipmunks. One was a modern shingled farmhouse with a sheltered porch cut into the roof, a spin on the Sea Ranch project, a family of jutting, zigzagging Bay Area retreats designed by Joseph Esherick, Jaffe's former boss. The other was a cut-out cubist fortress with the same plummeting, saltbox-style roof that would appear on the Becker House.

It was Becker who introduced Jaffe to the South Fork, and it was Becker who commissioned Jaffe's first conversation piece. Becker says he gave Jaffe four requirements for a weekend retreat on four acres of Wainscott pasture he bought for $36,000. The building had to have the rugged comfort of a farmhouse. All the materials had to be natural—no plaster or wall board for him. The sense of scale had to be robust. The communion with nature had to be organic; the indoors had to illustrate, accentuate and imitate the outdoors.

While designing Becker's peaceful pad, Jaffe's life was anything but peaceful. He was disturbed by the tragic death of his estranged wife, Barbara Cochran, whom he left in Illinois to join the Manhattan office of Philip Johnson, the fabled architectural minimalist. After Cochran was killed in a car crash in 1965, Jaffe reunited with their son, Miles, appearing without warning at the seven-year-old boy's grammar school, walking a dog he borrowed to seem more respectable on the playground. Father and son returned the dog to the pound and flew to a new life together in Manhattan, where they slept on a pull-out couch in Norman's office. Despite his rapidly rising fame, Jaffe scrambled to pay bills and avoid eviction. Miles recalls that "a big night out" with his dad was dinner at Tad's, a steak joint that specialized in $1.49 T-bones grilled by a window by 42$^{nd}$ Street.

Jaffe tried to make ends meet by playing ends against the middle. He illustrated fashion ads under the name Dave Dakota. He advertised fashions, and his firm, as a paid model in *Men's Bazaar*, a mod magazine. In a two-page photograph he reclined rakishly behind a scale model of his cascading Virginia house. His right hand rested on his left thigh, his right hand propped up his head, a strand of hair caressed his left eyebrow. He wore a turtleneck sweater and a Bill Blass twill suit, a very fashionable ensemble in the late sixties. He looked hip, dashing, ready for bear, lion and rhino. In fact, he looked like one of those supremely confident models in one of those "What Sort of Man Reads Playboy?" in-house ads.

"He looks like he's stepping out on the town when in fact he was really struggling to survive," says Miles Jaffe, who collaborated on his father's projects and who now designs furniture and houses. "He didn't even get to keep the jacket."

In the late sixties Jaffe suffered from chest pains that Miles attributes to the stress of being a single father and a solo architect. In 1968 father and son sought relief during a two-week vacation in the United Kingdom; according to Miles, Norman feared he was dying and wanted to visit the British Isles before his fear came true. The pair spent most of the trip in Ireland, where Jaffe found comfort in churches, castles and other sturdy, sacred buildings. He found inspiration in something most people would find uninspiring: a stone farmhouse with a collapsed gable in a meadow. That ruin became the Becker House's skeleton, and Jaffe's lightning/divining rod.

Back in America, Jaffe turned the Irish farmhouse every which way from Sunday. Fearlessly faithful to his reckless dreams, he visualized his belief that "you have to respect your insanity, or maybe an obsession that one can't immediately express." He outlined an abstract castle with a very solid, very prominent gable. He joined the façade to a low, long fence, leaving the silhouette of a sketchy sailboat. He placed the structure parallel to the road, to follow the horizontal flow of the pasture, maximize privacy and frame ocean views. He sheathed the shell in chunky, round stones, a rare material for East End houses but a plentiful material on East End beaches. Imported from the Delaware River region, the tawny, rusty rocks expressed Jaffe's belief that careful attention to natural details could create a sense of timelessness and other-worldliness.

Indeed, my planets shifted every day I watched masons build the Becker House's walls, cutting stones to fit on site, transforming a plain pasture into a lively quarry. The tall wall, I soon discovered, was quite vibrant. It hummed in the morning shadows, shouted in the afternoon sun, sang in the saffron light of early evening. At night it became a blue-black ghost pierced by a glowing doorway, a mesmerizing beacon on a road without street lamps. Decades later the torch-like effect helped me understand why my Irish relations were so thrilled when electricity came to their rural region in the fifties, when merely switching on a light in the dead of evening was an act of magic.

In the summer of 1969 it seemed I was the only one hypnotized by Jaffe's fantastic fantasy. Loitering in the one-room post office, which was around the corner from the Becker House, I heard locals denounce Jaffe's grand edifice as "a wall without a house," "a sheep shed," "a fucking folly." At the time I was too shy to set them straight. I was also too shy to walk the long driveway to the Becker House, knock on the door, and request a tour of my own personal sphinx. A budding purist, I worried that what was behind the walls wasn't nearly as exciting as the walls themselves, that behind that stone curtain the mighty Oz was really meek.

I finally saw all of the Becker House in the August 1972 edition of *House & Garden* magazine. The generous spread left me feeling as disappointed as Dorothy and her Yellow Brick Road gang. Behind the walls, the exterior looked cluttered and cramped—an avant-garde shed. The living room was awkwardly platformed to improve a view of the pasture and awkwardly wedged into a severely slanted space; low-slung windows above a built-in bench made the room a strange blend of cabin loft and airport lobby. The bolts and plates on the cedar beams were harshly industrial, the diagonal cedar planks on the walls chunky and clunky. The entire interior seemed imported from the Pacific Northwest, Jaffe's old stomping ground.

Still, there were many merits behind the walls. The oversized, erratically shaped shingles, hand split to fit on site, formed a delightfully barnacled tapestry. The pool sunk into the stone-paved terrace was elegantly austere. The rail-less staircase, set into a wall between master bedroom and loft, was a marvelously spiny sculpture. The loft was a funky crow's nest with a massive slanted skylight that offered a magnificent picture of the coast. The window somehow mimicked the viewfinder of a camera, an excellent illusion for an owner who used an antique view camera to shoot female landscapes.

Missing from the *House & Garden* spread were the unique problems of a unique building. Four decades later, Becker chuckles at the skylight that leaked and heated the loft like an oven. "That skylight was a nightmare," he says. "I can say this: When you do an architecturally designed one-of-a-kind house, you get magic—in the aesthetics, in the spatial qualities. But any time an architect builds a one-of-a-kind, you have all sorts of headaches. When I go to bed at night I want to be thinking about creative problems in my work; I don't want to be thinking about creative solutions to problems in my house. Now, if the architect had done a second and third version of the place . . ."

Jaffe lived with these faults in the summer of 1972, when he and his son bunked in the Becker House while their Norman-designed Bridgehampton home, with a bedroom designed by Miles, was being built. According to Becker, the architect shrugged off problems as the price of innovation. When clients nagged him about fixing flaws, Jaffe liked to repeat what Frank Lloyd Wright told a client who nagged him about repairing a leaky ceiling: "Get a bucket."

The Becker House was Jaffe's first stone building, his first landmark, his first trademark. In 1971 it was designated a Record building by *The Architectural Record*, a prestigious monthly. It also impressed Chico Hamilton, a renowned jazz drummer, bandleader and composer who was Becker's friend and colleague. The Becker House "was intriguing; it had a lot of mystery," says Hamilton, who met Jaffe in the fifties when he was playing with the Gerry Mulligan Quartet and the architect was studying at the University of California, Berkeley. "It was Harold."

In the early seventies Hamilton hired Jaffe to design his vacation home in the Springs, one of East Hampton's woodiest, earthiest sections. Before building began, Jaffe told Hamilton to sell the land and buy a splashier site, one more suitable for the architect's grand plan. Jaffe's Wright-like dictator act pissed off Hamilton, a major player who toured six years with singer Lena Horne, led a seminal West Coast quintet and owned a company that scored commercials and films. He shot down Jaffe with a jazzy colloquialism: "Fuck you, man!"

Hamilton kept his Springs lot. Jaffe spruced and spiced up the property by creating a vividly geometric saltbox with a tower, a floating deck, a suspended walkway to the garage and lots of glass to animate an already splendid view of the water. The project turned client and architect into good friends. Four decades later, Hamilton still enjoys his tree-beach house, and still savors his bond

The author's first favorite house, a Tudor-on-the-rocks in New Rochelle, N.Y., that his father sold to build a home in Wainscott. *(Gehman Family Collection)*

with its designer. "At this stage of the game, if you have a Jaffe house, it's a classic," he says. "I think my place is still dynamite. It's still a Jaffe special. It still has Norman's spirit."

The Becker House made me a Jaffe fan and critic. I admired the snaking roof of his Krieger House (Montauk, 1976), which simulated a shingled ramp to the sky and sea. I hemmed and hawed over his Lloyds House (East Hampton, 1978), a curious, cranky imitation of an airport terminal in New Mexico—or the futuristic island command headquarters of a James Bond villain. (It fares better in the film "The Door in the Floor" as the residence of a rich, revengeful model for a rude artist.) I never warmed up to his Further Lane House (East Hampton, 1980), an assortment of sloping, sharply angled roofs that resembles an origami ski lodge.

The Becker House taught me that rule-bending buildings can change your mental space, your compass, your perception of the relationship between nature and human nature. It made me an architecture fiend; over the next two decades I was possessed by crafty, crazy buildings all over the South Fork. A saltbox with a loft. A cement factory converted into a residential studio. A potato barn converted into a baronial bunker. Cottages made by carpenters for whaling ships. A whale-shaped church. A Greek Revival mansion looming over a gas station. A 20-foot-high cement duck, opened in 1931 as a poultry store and a roadside sphinx.

It took me 33 years, but I finally solved the riddle posed by my own personal sphinx. After a second phone conversation with Becker, I suddenly realized that the Becker House was kin to my first favorite home, a 1920s Tudor built into a cliff-cave in New Rochelle that my father bought in 1962 and sold in 1966 to finance our Wainscott residence. In that Tudor-on-the-rocks I imagined myself as a cowboy in the Sierra Nevadas, printed Play-Doh comic strips in a secret cubbyhole, met my newborn sister for the first time and shared some of my parents' happiest days together. It was my castle, my fortress, my imaginarium.

## THE STAR

The January 4, 1968 edition of *The East Hampton Star* led off with the tale of a theft at the Sagaponack home of Truman Capote, author of *In Cold Blood*, the sensational nonfiction novel about a Kansas community held hostage by the senseless execution of a wealthy farm family. Blending reporting with yarning, *Star* writer Jack Graves cast the robbers as Stooge-like saps who stuffed their booty, including bottles of 50-year-old bonded bourbon, into pillowcases, including one stamped "Capote," and left the loot in their cars for the cops to claim. He even took a swipe at the victim of the crime: "Though he wears sunglasses and is below average height, Mr. Capote cuts a striking figure."

You didn't need to read the headline—"In Hot Pursuit: Novel Non-Fiction"—to know Graves was subtly spoofing Capote's boast that *In Cold Blood* was a novel marriage of fact and fiction. I didn't need to know the article was a mild satire to be hooked line and sinker. Slowly and slyly, Graves put me in the misguided minds of the thieves, one of whom stole an Instamatic camera and a hi-fi as Christmas gifts for his wife. He made me chuckle along with the arresting and booking police officers, whose Christmas gift was an enormously entertaining robbery.

The Capote caper gave me two gifts. I learned that a fairly bloodless newspaper story can be a full-blooded adventure, a valuable lesson for a future feature writer. And I became a fan of *The Star*'s robust mix of local color, cheeky wit and panoramic perspective. The weekly paper, I soon discovered, was a general store of essential information, an almanac of folksy wisdom, a correspondence course of colorful citizenship.

*The Star* took its motto "The Star Shines for All" seriously. Most publications treat photographs as third-class citizens, the shabby cousins of stories. *Star* pictures were stand-alone stars. Used generously and exquisitely, they illustrated the South Fork's mercurial geography and illuminated its sublime beauty. In any given week you could see a moonlit beach underlined by lines from Matthew Arnold's poem "Dover Beach," the noble door of a distressed cottage built by a carpenter who built whaling ships, lobster pots masquerading as Claes Oldenburg hard sculpture.

It was editor Everett Rattray who decided *The Star* needed picturesque pictures. A native of East Hampton and a lover of East End wildlife, he knew that beautiful images of sand patterns and horses prancing in the snow could boost circulation—not

Window of *The East Hampton Star*, the weekly newspaper that willed and groomed the author to be a journalist. *(Photo by Bill Hayward)*

only subscriptions but heartbeats, too. Indeed, *The Star*'s photos became my magnetic map to the South Fork. They made me explore places I otherwise wouldn't have explored: Sag Harbor's fishtailing side streets; Georgica Pond's crooked creeks; the necklace of jeweled waterways—ponds, lakes, bays, harbors—from Montauk to Southampton.

If *The Star*'s photos were a map, the paper's letters to the editor were a town meeting. Every week I perused two facing broadsheets of opinions about pretty much everything under the stars and sun. In this gatefold/gateway you could read about a ban on miniskirts and a mini-history of beached whales, a poem about a strawberry festival and a poem from a Vietnam soldier requesting respect. There was even a fiery debate over the firing of a head librarian starring Jean Stafford, the short-story writer and novelist, and Dwight Macdonald, the editor, critic and professional radical.

There was so much variety because *The Star* had an open-door policy on letters to the editor. The paper published everything except messages deemed obscene, libelous, invasive and/or anonymous rants. Rattray liked to call the pages of missives "freedom hall," says his widow, Helen, then a *Star* reporter and now the paper's publisher. "He always had a more than tolerant streak for eccentrics," she adds, "and would sometimes say something to the effect of 'Who are we to decide who is crazy or not?'"

Ev Rattray admitted that sometimes he stretched his guidelines, printing letters "likely to get us sued" or with a point that "completely escapes us." He was certainly confused and amused by the paper's most clever, incomprehensible correspondent. Montauk resident Charles Chauncey "C. C." Pool fancied himself the East End's e. e. cummings, the ringmaster of a flea circus of codes. One of his favorite acts was castigating the Ladies' Village

Improvement Society, which in 1895 became East Hampton's aesthetic caretakers. Pool didn't care that the ladies preserved the village's award-winning beauty by launching a planning board and blocking billboards. To him, they were nothing more than fashionable fascists. In one letter he imagined his car—"my flying submarine"—leaving tire treads "upon the alabaster epidermises" of the LVIS queens—"our current Hamptons Dowage-Diumvirate."

Many of the tensions that Pool mocked were satirized in Marvin Kuhn's canny, uncanny cartoons. A land surveyor by profession, the native of Garden City, Long Island, surveyed local conflicts through two East Hampton fishing buddies in bib overalls, hip boots and eye-hiding hats. These Bonackers, or "Bubs," flouted authority by playing shuffleboard on freshly painted double yellow lines on the Montauk Highway. They silently criticized absurdly anal regulations, staring in bewilderment at a totem pole of beach signs prohibiting everything from sleeping to artists.

Kuhn's drawing was charmingly sketchy. In fact, when he became *The Star*'s cartoonist in 1964, he had never actually drawn a cartoon. Ev Rattray excused his fairly rough draftsmanship because Kuhn was a fellow Navy vet, sailor, fisherman and friend of local baymen. Kuhn, he quickly learned, was a skilled translator who could make taciturn, marble-mouthed Bonackers talk like town trustees ("I don't know which is worse . . . gypsy moths or groupers") or hippies ("It's simple, man—love is your bag—mine is fish"). His comic ventriloquism was a sly tribute to the Bubs, some of whom gave him free fish that kept his family afloat during his early lean years on the East End.

Kuhn's cartoons topped a long list of *The Star*'s curious quirks. Founded in 1885, the paper had the clout to compel its hometown to change its name from Easthampton to East Hampton. Its circulation was small: 7,500 in the winter, 9,000 in the summer. Yet its fan club was pretty powerful. "I reach for *The Star*," said political pundit Art Buchwald in a subscription ad, "like a drowning man grabbing for a life preserver."

*The Star* was fairly rare: a paper run by relatives who treated readers as relations. Jeannette Edwards Rattray became editor and publisher after the 1954 death of her husband, Arnold, who bought the weekly in 1935. A member of one of East Hampton's oldest families, and the grandchild of one of the South Fork's last deep-sea whaling captains, she was an unusual combination of civic impresario, tastemaker and social sociologist. Her column, which she began in the late thirties and wrote in a house behind *The Star*, was a cornucopia of local history, genealogy, books, films, fashions, architecture, blueblood parties, red-carpet premieres and verbal slide shows of her vacation-research trips. Her status as community figurehead and original native entitled her to end "Looking Them Over" not with her name but "One of Ours," a title she borrowed from one of Willa Cather's novels about Great Plains pioneers. Cather's book was published in 1922, two years before Rattray began her own frontier experience as the only woman reporter for an American paper in Shanghai.

Rattray considered herself a "sort of liaison between Main Street and the big world outside." Her son, Ev, reinforced this bridge when he became *The Star*'s editor in 1958 after receiving a master's degree in journalism. In addition to printing poetic photographs and wacky poem-letters, he significantly expanded coverage of the East End's fragile ecosystems. In the late 1960s to early '70s the paper covered the waterfront of hot-stove debates:

Jetties vs. beach erosion. Tern nests vs. dune buggies. Gypsy moths vs. trees. Groupers vs. families. Year-rounders vs. renters. Natives vs. Johnny-come-latelys, also known as "Coney Islanders."

Written and edited in a former pharmacy on Main Street, *The Star* dispensed strong medicine. Rattray began editorializing against the Vietnam War in 1962, when editors of much bigger papers were paying lip service to the conflict. He regularly made his column an ombudsman's office, explaining why *The Star* had to print stories of local soldiers in Vietnam as well as "serious arrests and other transgressions." On his watch *The Star* leveled the playing field of class, narrowing the gap between farmers and power brokers. The paper banned the occupations of parents from wedding announcements (although Ev endorsed his mother's wish to write what brides wore) and reduced celebrities to residents with flashy credits. In a caption for a photo promoting a benefit tennis tournament, Dustin Hoffman was described not as the star of "The Graduate" but as an actor who grew a summer beard to disguise his fame.

"What Ev and I would tell people was that East Hamptoners— Bonackers, if you will—were still close to their roots as honest, hardworking farmers and fishermen," says Helen Rattray, who runs *The Star* with editor David Rattray, her and Ev's son. "Their values and open-mindedness came along with their genes. What made people great had nothing to do with wealth but with the way they expressed their values. East Hampton became, for example, a place where homosexuals were able to settle because East Hamptoners were tolerant. *The Star* ran items about celebrities only when they did something locally or wrote a book. *Newsday* thought it was reverse snobbism. But I would hardly call adherence to Old Testament beliefs snobbish."

Ev is summarized neatly by his friend Tom Paxton—guitarist, singer, songwriter ("Ramblin' Boy," "The Last Thing on My Mind"), former East Hampton resident and onetime regular *Star* subject. "Ev ran *The Star* with a great sense of honor," says Paxton, who ice boated with Rattray. "He took his work with the paper very seriously, and himself lightly."

Rattray's balance was reflected in *The Star*'s photos, news stories and features. All the columnists, for example, were personal and communal, elegant and witty, cosmopolitan and country. In "The Fifth Column" Rattray often wrote about his rituals: fishing, sailing, escaping holiday traffic jams on the two-lane Montauk Highway. When taking back-road shortcuts, he warned, beware of "natives armed with bows, arrows and disputatious dispositions." One week Arthur J. Roth devoted "From the Scuttlehole" to locking himself in a car trunk and pleading with his dog to free him, a la Lassie. Another week he recalled spying on English police barracks for the Irish Republican Army—a plot in his novel *A Terrible Beauty*, which became a film starring Robert Mitchum. A Renaissance autodidact, Roth wrote children's books and renovated low-end houses bought by middle-class journalists like Jack Graves, who envied his colleague's ability to drop off the edge of the earth after dropping off 16 summer columns.

Another reason *The Star* felt like a neighborhood paper was that three of its freelance writers were my neighbors. Wainscott correspondent Laura Montant, who lived on Two Rod Highway, described the hamlet's comings, goings and stayings—everything from potato harvests to a strawberry-festival square dance. The beat was natural for a former staffer at *The New York World-Telegram*, where she covered horse shows and operas, Margaret Mead and Eleanor Roosevelt. Her husband, Philippe, a professional photographer, frequently took pictures for *The Star*; he was on Two Rod Highway when he snapped one of my family's favorite portraits of my sister.

*The Star* launched the journalism career of Florence Fabricant, who lived a few hundred yards from us on Roxbury Lane. An avid cook, she relished making meals with fresh products as local as her backyard: wild raspberries in the woods by Wainscott North West Road, small potatoes gleaned from fall harvests along Wainscott's Main Street, crabs caught in newly pesticide-free Georgica Pond. A former marketing researcher for an advertising firm, she marketed herself as a food writer to Ev Rattray, who agreed to pay her $25 per piece when she would have accepted $5.

Introduced in May 1972, Fabricant's "In Season" column chronicled picking and cooking, buying and informing. Her writing quickly impressed Alden Whitman, a South Fork resident and a *New York Times* reporter best known for pioneering the paper's interview-based, personalized obituaries. Whitman featured Fabricant in a September 1972 article in *The Times'* Long Island section, paving the way for her to write for *The Times* along with *The Star*. Her two journalism lives united one evening in 1974 when she and her husband Richard hosted Whitman, Helen Rattray and Ev Rattray at their Wainscott house. That night Ev received a telephone call telling him his mother was about to die. Rattray and Whitman then spent a half hour outdoors plotting *The Times'* obit for Jeannette Rattray, who died from a cerebral hemorrhage, also Willa Cather's fate.

Jake Murray, who lived between Fabricant and Montant on Foxcroft Lane, was *The Star*'s roving rogue. He wrote about a

Southampton judge who let businesses open on Sundays and the pros and cons of X-rated films at the Bridgehampton drive-in. He mocked Puritans who crusaded against sex on the beach, joking that skinny dipping at night is dangerous only because "you can't see your date in the surf." He shamelessly plugged his 1969 novel *The Devil Walks on Water*, disclosing that he sent copies to Lillian Hellman, Howard Hughes and other bold-faced names.

In 1970 Jake was profiled by Jack Graves, my favorite *Star* writer. A native of the Pittsburgh suburb of Sewickley, Graves began working at the weekly in October 1967, replacing a reporter killed in a car crash. He soon discovered he was hired more for the quantity of his stories than their quality. Ev Rattray was apparently impressed by the seven daily articles he sometimes wrote for *The Long Island Press* while his mentor played golf.

Rattray immediately gave Graves a column, a reward usually awarded to veterans. Graves rewarded Rattray's faith by becoming *The Star*'s busiest, most versatile writer—the paper's Swiss Army knife. Graves covered the town board and the town trustees; the bulldozing of the channel between the Atlantic Ocean and Georgica Pond; the making of "Maidstone," Norman Mailer's ad-lib film featuring boxer Jose Torres. He reviewed books and plays, took photographs and analyzed an annual charity softball game between teams of well-known artists and writers. He was there when second baseman Saul Bellow and shortstop Neil Simon formed a literary Hall of Fame double-play tandem, and he was there when artist Herman Cherry tossed a softball-painted grapefruit that writer George Plimpton pulverized.

Like *The Star*'s other star writers, Graves had a snappy, *New Yorker*-esque sense of humor. When a haiku writer criticized him for criticizing her images, he defended himself in an editor's-note haiku: "Poetic license covered/Deborah's haiku as the/Grass the field mice."

More than any of *The Star*'s star writers, Graves considered the community his clamshell. His "Point of View" column was a true journal of his life, with entries about his tennis-playing prowess in the Army, his hearing loss and his new hammock. He interviewed everyone and anyone for his profiles, published under the headings "The Star Talks To" and "The Star Goes To." He had the knack of gently, jovially helping subjects find their way through thickets of ideas, whether the subjects were Dwight Macdonald or a tree surgeon-sculptor, Tom Paxton or kite-flying Cub Scouts.

Graves helped me find my journalistic compass, leaving me with three key tips. One, everyone has a story worth sharing in public. Two, a good story is really a good conversation between a good talker and an equally good listener. And, three, never, ever underestimate the power of passionate rambling and creative lying.

In October 1971 Graves began his splashiest assignment. That month he accompanied health inspectors on a raid of Grey Gardens, a ramshackle mansion and feral estate in one of East Hampton's plushest neighborhoods. During "the unique house tour" he met Edith Bouvier Beale ("Big Edie") and her same-named daughter ("Little Edie"), who lived with no running water, mounds of trash, diseased cats, feline feces and raccoons that crawled through a hole in the roof. Parked in the jungle-like frontyard of their once-pristine property was a 1937 Cadillac, a shrine to the late Mr. Beale and his frequent driving companion, a Dalmation named, naturally, Spot.

The Edies dubbed their décor "Louisiana Bayou." Their neighbors were neither impressed nor amused by this swamp by the sea. The Beales, they complained to the town patriarchs, were spoiling and soiling their hydrangea walls, golf-course lawns and rarefied airs.

The Beales quickly became international icons, the Beatles of East Hampton. What made their story so juicy was that the Edies were the aunt and first cousin of Jacqueline Bouvier Kennedy Onassis, widow of a president and wife of a billionaire. What made their story so memorable was Graves' bittersweet Dickensian spin. He portrayed the Beales as Miss and Mrs. Havisham, relentlessly independent, ruthlessly articulate kin caught in the crosshairs of class warfare. "East Hampton is such a mean place," Little Edie told him. "It's perfectly gorgeous on the surface and underneath I don't think anybody's human."

In 1972 the Beales' dilemma became more humane. That year Jackie O and her sister, Lee Radziwill, paid to repair and stabilize Grey Gardens, saving the Edies from eviction and their home from extinction. The pilgrimage spurred "Grey Gardens," a 1975 documentary by Albert and David Maysles, directors of such daring films as "Salesman" and "Gimme Shelter." Their movie, in turn, spawned "Grey Gardens" the 2006 Broadway musical and "Grey Gardens" the 2009 HBO feature starring Jessica Lange and Drew Barrymore.

Four decades later, Graves remains modest about breaking the South Fork saga of the decade. "The story found us," he points out, "not the other way around." He admits his zest for a zinging tale was diminished by his compassion for the Beales as victims of gestapo-like inspectors. In fact, shortly after the raid on Grey Gardens, the same neo-fascists raided a residential nursery school run by his future landlady.

Graves declined to see the "Grey Gardens" documentary when it premiered in 1976 in East Hampton. He nodded his head when a Maysles brother asked: "Too real for you, Jack?" He did, however, honor the Edies with a homegrown, overgrown installation. Tickled by their 1937 Cadillac garden sculpture, he let his 1967 "baby puke" Ford Falcon rot in his frontyard "for quite a while before yielding to decorum."

It was this one-two punch of guts and graciousness that made Graves the first journalist who made me want to be one. More than anyone at *The Star* or my other news schools—*The New York Times*, *Life* magazine, "60 Minutes"—he convinced me that journalism should be serious and fun—serious fun. That a feature writer should be somewhere between a king and a servant. And that the middle of nowhere—be it Sagaponack, N.Y., or Holcomb, Ks., or Old Zionsville, Pa.—is often the center of everything.

# Battery Mates

The author received this autographed photo of his baseball hero Carl
Yastrzemski from Yaz's parents during a 1968 dinner at the Gehman
home in Wainscott. *(Gehman Family Collection)*

# MIKE & ME

I met my first full-fledged friend on my first full day in Wainscott. My father was driving around on a Saturday morning in June 1967, giving me the lay of the land, when he pulled over to watch boys playing baseball on the field along Wainscott Hollow Road, near the cemetery and the one-room school. Dad knew there was nothing like baseball to comfort a kid in a new community, so he introduced me to Joe Raffel, manager of the brand-spanking-new Wainscott Wildcats. Joe then introduced me to his outfielder son, Mike, who had an ear-to-ear grin that can only be described as wicked. I took one look at that shit-kicking smile and just knew we'd be the South Fork's answer to Huck Finn and Tom Sawyer.

Our adventures began that day on that wacky field. Before we began playing, Mike showed me the quirks of a rectangle only 38 steps wide and littered by weeds, stones and sandy patches. He told me to hit balls up the middle, so they wouldn't end up foul on the road or in the cemetery. Get ready, he said, for crazy bounces that made balls skip over gloves and sail over shoulders. Be prepared for baseball as pinball.

Mike's patient tutorial made me, the Wildcats' only non-local, feel like a local. His simple act of kindness quickly closed a gap between different kids from different worlds. I was the suburban son of a Manhattan advertising executive. He was the rural son of a lineman for the Long Island Lighting Company. I lived with a sibling in a pretty calm house. He lived with four siblings in a pretty rowdy house. I was scarecrow skinny, with pale skin that tanned and dirty-blonde hair that bleached at the beach. He had the solid body of a catcher, with auburn hair and a welter of freckles, Celtic features he inherited from his mother, the former RoseMarie Boyle.

We soon learned we shared much more than our mothers' Irish backgrounds and our fathers' rugged noses. We were born 66 days apart, had recently played the outfield as Little League rookies and were coached by our fathers to be aggressive and smart. We took pride in rounding bases tightly, charging grounders, treating the cut-off man's mitt as a bull's-eye.

Mike Raffel, the author's first full-fledged friend, baseball teammate/rival, rock 'n' roll guru and Huck Finn ally. *(Photo courtesy of Mike Raffel)*

Mike and I didn't care that the Wildcats weren't wild. Our only opponent was a Sag Harbor team managed by one of Joe Raffel's coworkers. Joe not only coached us, he bought our bats, balls and uniforms. His biggest challenge was fielding a complete squad of nine boys during the seductive summer. He bought soda and ice cream as extra bonuses to drag kids from body surfing, weeding fields and other warm-weather rituals.

My friendship with Mike was quickly and severely tested by, of all things, baseball. He worshipped the New York Yankees, the archenemy of my favorite team, the Boston Red Sox. That summer a bloody rivalry turned bloodier as the Sox rose from ninth place to win their first pennant in 21 years and the Yankees finished in ninth place, three years after losing the World Series. For Mike, the wound was salted by the rise of Carl Yastrzemski, the young Sox left fielder from Bridgehampton, and the fall of Mickey Mantle, the Yanks' legendary center fielder. Mike was too much of a Mantle fan to cheer for Yaz, even though Yaz was a fellow Polish-American from the East End.

Now, I was a very stubborn kid, born under the sign of Taurus. Mike's bullheadness, however, put him in another league, another universe; by comparison, I was a mere lamb. My new best friend spent the entire summer and fall of 1967, as well as the winter of 1968, disputing the indisputable fact that the Sox dominated the Yanks—that my team was his team's daddy and mommy. Mike's one and only argument was that the Sox's sudden success was a freak, baseball's version of Halley's Comet. The Yanks, he said gleefully, had won 20 championships since the Sox had won their last one back in prehistoric 1918. Besides, shit, man, Yaz could have a half-dozen more career years and still remain unworthy of carrying Mantle's jock strap.

Mike and I entertained ourselves by debating the merits of our teams' best players. We butted heads over first basemen (George Scott vs. Joe Pepitone), center fielders (Reggie Smith vs. Tom Tresh), pitchers (Jim Lonborg vs. Mel Stottlemyre). We called each other all the bad words we knew: "idiot," "chump," "dickhead." We never really meant the curses. In fact, we were the very models of agreeable disagreeability. Hell, we could have taken our act on the road, proving to the world that Sox and Yank fans can piss each other off and still stay pals.

We built our friendship, in fact, around creative competition. We weren't content to merely body surf waves to shore; we had to be bruised, battered sumo wrestlers of the sea. For us, playing normal tennis was for wimps; we served and volleyed by a condemned beach house to a tape of "Hot Pants," "Sex Machine" and other James Brown funk classics.

Our best battleground was the basketball court on Foxcroft Lane, an extension of the Raffels' driveway. The plywood backboard, made by Joe Raffel, hung on a telephone pole with an electric light he installed without permit or permission. Wainscott's only street lamp south of the Montauk Highway allowed us to play past midnight, until our palms were black and cracked.

Like the rectangular baseball field, the Foxcroft court was a mine field that demanded constant care. We had to stop short on drives to the basket to avoid smacking the unpadded, splintered pole. We tiptoed on drives along the baseline to avoid spraining an ankle in the rut between the street and the rhododendron den in front of Jake Murray's house-studio. Shooting from the corner required angling the ball over trees and telephone wires; hours and hours of practice made us deadly from behind the backboard.

The court, in short, was as regulation as we wanted it to be. So were our games. Sometimes we imitated players in one-on-one competitions televised during halftime of NBA matches. We particularly liked guys with street flash: Nate "The Skate" Archibald, as quick as a hummingbird; Connie "Hawk" Hawkins, famous for his windmill dunks; "Pistol Pete" Maravich, who spiced fast breaks by whipping passes between his legs and his opponent's legs. We embellished "H-O-R-S-E," a free-style, top-this-sucker contest, with our own versions of the NBA's snazziest moves: Dick Barnett's leg-kicking fadeaway jumper; Jerry Lucas's chest-high, heaving bombs; Kareem Abdul-Jabbar's sweeping sky hook; Dave Cowens's sudden baseline spin, which allowed the 6-foot-9 center to beat the 7-foot-2 Jabbar to the basket.

Mike introduced me to an absolutely filthy defensive move. When I went up for a jump shot, and he was out of position, he bent over, dropping his head to around my waist. Worried I would fall over him, I became distracted and, more often than I care to remember, clanged the ball off the rim.

I introduced Mike to trash talk from the mean suburban courts of New Rochelle. After swishing a shot, I'd wag a finger at him and shout "In yo' face!" or, better yet, "Face!" There was nothing more satisfying than talking smack to Mike, who was one of the South Fork's best smack attackers.

The woofing continued in the basement of Mike's house, which we turned into a hippie comedy club. We laughed our fool heads off listening to records of such riotous routines as George Carlin's "Seven Words You Can Never Say on Television" and Cheech & Chong's "Sister Mary Elephant." We busted a gut mimicking Sister Mary, the mousy teacher who, failing to silence

The author, left, and Mike Raffel watch a 1968 game between their respective favorite teams, the Boston Red Sox and the New York Yankees, at Yankee Stadium; sitting in back are Mike's parents, Rosie and Joe, who made him wear a tie. *(Gehman Family Collection)*

her noisy students with "Class . . . Class . . . ," shuts them up by screaming "SHUDDUUUUUUPPP!" Mike, a Catholic schooler, enjoyed mocking a humorless nun. I enjoyed letting my freak flag fly, which gave me a dope high without the dope.

Mike did his own routines between routines. He knocked me out with his impersonation of the Bonackers, an extended clan of anglers, clammers, painters and carpenters living around Accabonac

Harbor in the Springs section of East Hampton. Mike pronounced "pie" like "poy," ended every other sentence with "Yessiree, Bub!" and generally nailed the chewy, marbled, New England/England talk of the "Bubbies." He seasoned the act by shuffling his feet and sucking an imaginary chaw of grass. He was a complete wickus, which is Bonac for "rascal."

In that same cellar Mike became my rock 'n' roll guru. Before I met him, I was a rock altar boy. I liked the Beatles because of their cartoon series; the Monkees' TV show made me want to start a band. I could have used someone like Mike's Uncle Denny, who babysat his nephew in the homes of friends with great record collections. Guided by Mike, I roamed the rock tributaries of acid, country, funk, glam, metal and psychedelic. We rolled with the Allman Brothers and rambled with the Stones; chanted Paul Revere and the Raiders' "Cherokee Nation" and screamed Three Dog Night's "Joy to the World"; debated guitar gods (Jimi Hendrix vs. Jimmy Page) and group names (Blue Oyster Cult vs. Black Oak Arkansas); drooled over the naked women on the sleeve of "Electric Ladyland" and the naked girl holding a phallic model plane on the cover of "Blind Faith."

It was in that sonic romper room that I fell for Mott the Hoople, the first band I swore I discovered. Ian Hunter and his mates seduced me with the funky boogie of "All the Way to Memphis," the greasy pyramidal power of "Rock 'n' Roll Queen," the crunching march of "All the Young Dudes." I dug Hunter's endearing sneer, the way he mocked and mourned rock excesses in "The Saturday Kids" and "Ballad of Mott the Hoople." His sunglasses, top hat and scary hair gave him the appearance of a carnival ringleader and sideshow, a suitable combination for the star of a group named after a novel starring a circus freak.

Hunter had a knack for exposing the freak in all of us. He showcased his bittersweet resignation in "I Wish I Was Your Mother," the mandolin-caressed confession of an outsider who yearns to be an insider. The narrator curses his girlfriend's beauty yet wishes he could have grown up with her, playing with her siblings, joining a family "for a while." I felt like the narrator's younger brother; like him, I seesawed between confidence and doubt, belonging and not belonging, geekdom and dudedom.

To me, Mike was the quintessential young dude. I envied his guts the way Tom Sawyer envies Huck Finn's. I wished I had the balls to leave my house late at night to call a girlfriend from the phone booth outside the post office. I wished I had the cojones to shoot birds by the Georgica Association's tennis court, then hide behind hedgerows to outfox The Settlement's easily outfoxed guard.

While I practiced mischief in Mike's house, it took five years for his mischief to really rub off on me. One day in 1972 I accepted a dare to stand by the picture window of the Brothers Four pizzeria in East Hampton and scratch my chin with my finger tips. Then I ran like hell down an alley to escape the knife-wielding brother who wanted to mince me like garlic for flashing the universal Italian sign for "Fuck you and all the whores in your house, too."

I like to think I gave Mike a small slice of freedom. I offered him my house as a rare retreat, a no-chore zone. He could eat from dishes he didn't have to wash, play ping-pong without being pestered by younger siblings and their friends, peek at *Playboy*s without punishment—as long as we were in the family room and my father wasn't.

Looking back, I feel a bit guilty I spent far more time at Mike's place than he spent at mine. I feel worse that our parents never socialized together. The gulf seems absurd considering our families lived a street apart and we were close enough to be brothers. My guess is that Joe and Rosie Raffel were too busy working and raising kids, while my mother was too shy and my father too snobby. The only time our dads got together outside Wainscott was at Yankee Stadium. That day the Yanks played the Sox, naturally.

Despite rooting for each other's archenemy, Mike and I had only one wicked argument. I was pissed at him when I learned he ditched me when a friend of his kidnapped him on a double date, during which Mike fooled around with a girl in a car on Sag Harbor's Long Wharf. My anger didn't even last the night. In fact, I forgot the incident for over 30 years, remembering only when Mike reminded me. I probably forgot because I felt bad for him after his mother gave him holier hell. Rosie reamed her son so good, he couldn't separate the shit from the fan.

I can't thank Mike enough for four lifelong lessons. One, the foundation of friendship is acceptance. Two, rock 'n' roll can chase any blues. Three, you need only two guys for a gang. And, four, a Yankee fan can remain friends with a Red Sox fan even when the Yankee fan is still sore at the Red Sox fan, four decades later, for winning his Mickey Mantle cards.

# YAZ, DAD & ME

You never forget your first pennant race. I was baptized in 1967 when the Boston Red Sox rose from Davy Jones' basement to win the American League championship. They were basically willed from ninth place to the World Series by Carl Yastrzemski, who had a career year bordering on the mythic. He led the league in batting average, home runs and runs batted in. He led the majors in clutch hits, catches and throws. And he led the world in making kids like me baseball fans forever.

It was my father who actually made me a Yastrzemski fan. In the winter of 1966 he enlivened a boring visit to check the construction of our Wainscott house with a side trip to Yastrzemski's childhood home on School Street in Bridgehampton. Parked near a Little League field, Dad proceeded to tell me a real-life baseball fable about a son and a father.

It was the story of a boy named Carl whose father, also named Carl, gave him a toy baseball bat when he was 18 months old. Who in the winter practiced his swing in the garage with a lead bat and a sheepskin coat. Who played on three teams with and against his dad, who hit so well, even in his 40s, that he was called a right-handed version of Ted Williams, the Red Sox Hall of Famer with a lofty lifetime batting average of .344. Who in 1961 replaced Williams in left field after signing a six-figure contract negotiated by his father, a potato farmer who had never earned more than $10,000 a year. Who won a batting title in his fifth season, turned Fenway Park's 37-foot-high, 240-foot-wide left-field wall—"The Green Monster"—into his personal playground and became a New England folk hero known simply as Yaz.

Larry Gehman in his late 20s, wearing the uniform of his employer, Dan River Mills, ready for life's 3-2 sliders. *(Gehman Family Collection )*

Since my father was a lay preacher and an amateur sports psychologist, the tale was really a parable disguised as a pep talk. Yaz, he knew, would be a great role model during my first Little League season. Dad was so, so right. That spring I played left field because Yaz played left field. I pitched because Yaz pitched in high school, throwing two no-hitters in his senior year. I was better on the mound, where I tossed a shutout on my birthday, than in the outfield, where a fly ball bounced off my head after I lost it in the sun.

While I imitated Yaz, my father did his best impression of Yaz Sr. Dad was my catcher, my fungo hitter, my coach. He was even my umpire for an inning, replacing an ump who left a game early due to an emergency. Dressed in business shirt and tie, Dad stood behind the mound instead of the plate and made two controversial calls. I walked in a run on a ball I swore was a strike, then struck out a batter looking at a ball I swore was a ball. Afterward Dad bought me an ice cream, patted my shoulder and refused to apologize.

What my father didn't tell me is that it was a terrible time to root for Yaz and the Red Sox. In his six years the Sox had lost 101 more times than they had won, earning themselves the nickname the "Dead Sox." In 1966 they finished ninth, a half game from last place, under Yaz's fourth manager. Yaz batted an anemic .278, 34 points under his league-leading average in 1965. The steep drop, his second in three years, bolstered his reputation as an underachiever, a pretender to Ted Williams' throne. Williams routinely hit 30 to 40 home runs each season with a whip-smart swing, a scientific knowledge of the strike zone and a ripped, rippling 6-foot-3, 205-pound body. Yaz, a fellow left-handed batter, had never hit more than 20 homers in a season. His relatively small body (5-feet-11, 175–180 pounds) tired late in the season. He lunged at balls outside the strike zone, ignoring the advice of Williams, his occasional batting instructor, to patiently wait for the right pitch to pull and drive. Cast as Williams' successor, he strained to hit homers with a ferocious swing he developed to emulate Williams' power.

A much better fielder than Williams, Yaz had won two Gold Gloves, throwing out 19 runners in those years with a dead-eye arm and a deft ability to decoy, or deke, Fenway Park runners into a false sense of security, thinking a ball off the Green Monster was beyond his control when it wasn't. There were also two seasons when he made 11 errors, most of them on throws that sailed over bases, the result of overconfidence and misguided pride. Like Williams, he occasionally dogged it on the bases and in the field when a game was out of reach, two black eyes for a team captain.

Worst of all, Yaz shared Williams' lazy arrogance. He once told veteran pitcher Bill Monbouquette that he sometimes refused to hustle after balls ricocheting in Fenway's tricky left-field corner, where the foul line is only three feet from the jutting grandstand. Monbouquette, then Boston's unofficial cop, ripped Yaz a new one: "Let me tell you something, pal, they've run better players than you out of this town."

Yaz worried he'd be run out of town until January 1967, when Boston General Manager Dick O'Connell assured him he wouldn't be traded. Relieved that his job was secure, Yaz decided to rebuild his career by rebuilding his body. He hired a personal trainer, common today in professional baseball but rare in the sixties. A drill sergeant named Gene Berde, a former trainer for the Hungarian Olympic boxing team, put him through a punishing regimen of jumping rope, hitting a speed bag, pushing up on finger tips, stretching on a Swedish wall ladder, running in the snow and sprinting 60 yards 20 straight times. Berde, who was a packed 5-foot-6 and 160 pounds, goaded the bigger Yaz, calling him a weakling and a wimp, toughening him by insulting his toughness. He essentially returned Yaz to his training-camp childhood in his Bridgehampton garage, when he improved his eye-hand coordination by hitting a ball strung with fishing tackle with a lead bat up to 1,000 times a day.

Berde's boot camp worked wonders. Yaz entered the 1967 season with significantly more power, stamina, agility and will. He harnessed all these strengths in an April 14 game against the New York Yankees, Boston's archenemy. Billy Rohr of the Sox entered the ninth inning with a no-hitter, a remarkable feat for a rookie pitching his first game. Tom Tresh, the Yankee center fielder, led off with a wicked line drive that looked like it would sail over Yaz's head for the game's first hit. Yaz pivoted, ran back, leaped full out like a wide receiver, caught the ball over his shoulder in the web of his glove and held it as he belly flopped and somersaulted. Rather than relax on the grass, he popped up in two seconds and quickly threw the ball back to the infield, even though there was no one on base. Rohr lost the no-hitter an out later but the message was clear as crystal: The new Yaz was a missionary.

Always an exceptional left fielder, Yaz became a player possessed. He charged grounders and line drives with locomotive steam. He threw lasers to second base, turning many doubles into singles. He tamed Fenway Park's Green Monster, uncannily gauging the different paths of balls hitting concrete, rivets, 2-by-4s and a tin scoreboard with slots for changing numbers by hand, catching on the fly 36-foot-high pool-ball bounces and pin-ball caroms with backspin. He played angles so accurately and effortlessly, he seemed to turn Fenway's outfield into a jai-alai fronton.

That summer I imitated Yaz by throwing a tennis ball against the backboards of tennis courts I imagined as green monsters. I spent far more time copying his new, novel batting stance, which he started in May to stop a slump. Yaz cocked his left elbow at or just under ear level, placing his top hand on the same plane as the "B" on his helmet. He compensated for this crazily high alignment by throwing the rest of his body—and logic—out of whack. When the pitcher began winding up, he lifted his right foot about six inches and shifted his stance to the right, which gave him a fuller view of the delivery. As the ball approached the plate, he turned his hips toward the pitcher, which gave him better leverage to pull and drill the ball—Williams' most valuable tip. At the same time he dropped his hands quickly, yanked them back furiously and buzzsawed the bat through the strike zone. His improved dexterity and strength allowed him to murder letter-high fastballs he once fouled off or whiffed.

That summer I joined the legion of young Yaz clones. I adopted and adjusted his pre-at-bat rituals, rubbing my hands with dirt (or grass), hitching my pants (or shorts), patting my helmet (or hat). I raised the knob of the bat near my ears, flexed my right elbow (I was right handed), squinted my left eye and dared the pitcher to throw a high, hard one by me. I felt cool and mean, stoic and heroic. I felt like I was channeling Yaz's spirit. After all, I played at two Yaz shrines: the Little League field by his childhood home in

Bridgehampton and the rectangular field in Wainscott by a potato field owned by the Dankowskis, one of many Polish families who considered Yaz an ethnic elder.

The new Yaz inspired a young team led by a rookie manager. Every other day he seemed to rise to new heroics, most of which are seared into the memories of most true-blue Red Sox fans. That June Eddie Stanky, manager of the Chicago White Sox and an ornery cuss, dismissed Yaz as an all-star "from the neck down." Yaz retaliated by spanking Stanky's team with six hits in a doubleheader. Rounding the bases after a homer, he tipped his hat toward Stanky, a gentlemanly fuck-you-too. The gesture stood out because it came from a no-nonsense baseball businessman who usually ran out homers with head down.

Yaz inspired the Sox to recover from a devastating loss. On August 18 they were in a four-team race, separated by two games, when center fielder Tony Conigliaro—star slugger, New England native, fan favorite—had his left cheekbone shattered by a pitch from Jack Hamilton of the California Angels. The day after Tony C left the field on a stretcher, lost for the season, Yaz had four hits in a win against the Angels, one of the teams in the pennant chase. The day after that he hit two three-run homers as the Sox swept a doubleheader from the Halos, winning the nightcap 9–8 after trailing 8–0. Every day he seemed to have the play-by-play intensity of a middle linebacker, a quarterback, a field general.

By now the South Fork was Yaz Central. Grown men and women babbled about their homegrown hero in the post office, in the supermarket, on the beach, at the drive-in, even at the Bridgehampton store where I bought my comic books and horror-film magazines. Sharing this mania day by day, hour by hour, was unbelievably, off-the-Richter-scale exciting. For the first time in my life I felt plugged into a great community switchboard. For the first time I had a cause outside myself.

My father was amused and touched by my passion, which reminded him of his passion for the 1930s Philadelphia A's, one of the worst teams of all time. Dad fed my fever by introducing me to his singing pal Pete Michne, a postman who played the outfield with Yaz at Bridgehampton High. Michne, who shared Yaz's dark hair, sharp eyes and dominant nose, spun my head with stories of Yaz's youthful exploits: tape-measure homers; 26 straight hits; striking out 40 of 42 batters.

Dad treated me to several visits to the Village Restaurant in Bridgehampton, the epicenter of Yaz Central. The family business was owned and operated by Billy DePetris, a star pitcher on the Yaz/Michne team who that summer celebrated the success of Yaz and the Sox by hanging nearly 200 red socks around his eatery, in the process wiping out the local 5&10's supply of ruby hosiery. Billy had fairly dark skin, curly hair, an elephant's memory, an X-rated mouth and the theatrical flair of a natural-born raconteur—or snake-oil peddler. While my father drank beers and I sipped Shirley Temples, he regaled us—and everyone else within shouting distance—with tales of stickballing with Yaz behind the restaurant; playing six-man football with himself at quarterback and Yaz at halfback, and pitching knuckle curves to Carl Jr. until Carl Sr. ordered his son to save his body for the outfield and the major leagues.

DePetris was just as salty when I interviewed him in 2002 in his trailer home/Yaz museum in Flanders, outside Riverhead.

Then a cook for a Sag Harbor convent, he loudly, proudly recalled throwing six no-hitters in 13 high-school games ("Them guys didn't get a sneeze off me") and being the lone Italian on the otherwise all-Polish Bridgehampton White Eagles ("They called me 'hot dog' and 'greasy.' "). Carl Sr., he said, was a dictatorial coach, "a real Billy Martin guy" who talked strategy while raking the mound. "His ethic was: Work your ass off and you can leave this little punk-ass town."

Stoked by these stories, my father became my baseball benefactor. That summer he built me a pitcher's mound of dirt, sand and clay in our Wainscott backyard. He made a rubber from two bricks, turned a gardener's pillow into home plate and caught me with an oversized knuckleball catcher's mitt he bought with cigar wrappers. Dad showed me how to throw rising and sinking fastballs and a curve that broke from a batter's ass to the outside corner. A taskmaster in tennis and singing, he became a taskmaster in pitching, too. Every session I had to throw 10 balls around the letters, 10 around the knees, 10 on the left side of the plate and 10 on the right side. I relieved the boredom by thinking of Yaz throwing a tennis ball at a square on the garage behind his boyhood house on School Street.

Dad's most ingenious trick involved a cocktail. During every practice he placed a filled martini glass by his left thigh, daring me to control my control so he could control his thirst. I'm happy to report that while I broke his toe with a pitch, I never broke the glass.

Yaz fever continued after Labor Day, when we returned to New Rochelle for the school year. On September 18 his 40th homer tied a game against the Detroit Tigers, another pennant rival, in the ninth inning. Two days later his 41st homer helped beat the Cleveland Indians by a run. His devotion to winning practically burned a hole in the cover of the September 8 issue of *Life* magazine, where he ran with a grimace that was almost demonic.

On the last weekend the Sox were one of three teams separated by 1.5 games contending for a spot in the World Series. They played their final two games against the Minnesota Twins, who led the league by one game. We spent that last weekend in Wainscott so I could watch the games on the Sox's Connecticut station, another priceless gift from Dad.

That weekend Yaz graduated from hero to legend. In the next-to-last game he had three hits in four at-bats, including a key three-run homer, to help the Sox rally for a win and move into a first-place tie with the Twins. In the final game he went 4–4, tying the score in the sixth inning with a two-run single against Twins pitcher Dean Chance, one of his nemeses. I'll never forget the way he muscled the ball into center field, transforming a line drive into a missile. It was my first truly memorable, truly historic hit.

The Red Sox clinched a tie for the pennant when shortstop Rico Petrocelli caught the last out, a pop-up in shallow left field. Yaz charged behind him, hands held high, a rare burst of enthusiasm for a stoic. I jumped for joy on the sofa in our den, bending the springs. I bent them lower later that afternoon when the Angels beat the Tigers in the second game of a doubleheader, giving the Sox their first pennant in 21 years.

Yaz hit a remarkable .523 with five homers and 16 RBI over the final 12 games of a wild pennant chase. He finished the season with career highs in batting average (.326, five points better than his previous best), RBI (121, or 27 more than his best) and homers (44, topping his record by a whopping 24). He became only the 15$^{th}$ winner of baseball's fabled Triple Crown; it would be another 45 years before another major leaguer won another. He could have won a fourth crown for largely turning a team of losers into winners. He helped Jim Lonborg win 22 games after going 19–27 in his first two seasons. He helped second-year first baseman George Scott raise his average from .245 to .303. And he helped rookie manager Dick Williams, a former Boston infielder, succeed with a Marine-like program that included obsessive practice of the suicide squeeze, volleyball to limber up pitchers, and chewing out players—including Yaz—in public.

Yaz's fiery grace under tremendous pressure won him another accolade: lifelong respect from his peers. In 2002 I was breakfasting with Tony Oliva, the former Twins outfielder and batting champion, at a Pennsylvania inn where amateurs played baseball with and against former major leaguers. When I asked Oliva about Yaz in 1967 he rubbed his eyes, smiled sadly and groaned: "Oh man, Yaz was the *man* that year. Oh man, he *killed* us! Oh man, why did you have to go and ruin my appetite?"

Yaz's hunger for heroics continued in the World Series against the St. Louis Cardinals. He made a great leaping catch, hit three homers and helped the Sox win two straight games to eliminate a 3–1 deficit. In the seventh game he had one of three hits against the virtually unhittable Bob Gibson, who won his third game of the Series against an exhausted Lonborg, who had won two games and was starting on only two days' rest. Yaz's single in the ninth inning was greeted with a standing ovation by the Fenway faithful, a tingling thank-you for a Cinderella season.

After Gibson struck out Scott for the final out, I bawled like a baby. I received unexpected comfort from my normally tough-guy father, who made me cry tears of frustration by slaughtering me at tennis and ping-pong. Dad told me another real-life fable, this time about a rookie pitcher who overcame big-league adversity. Pete Naktenis finished 0–1 with a ghastly 12.54 ERA in seven games for the 1936 Philadelphia A's, who finished an abysmal 53–100. Naktenis didn't return to the majors until 1939, when he compiled a nifty 2.25 ERA in three games for the Cincinnati Reds. The moral of the story? If Pete Naktenis could bounce back, so can you.

Dad was so, so right again. I forgot my grief the next day when Mike Raffel, my best friend and Yankee-loving rival, mocked me for being a poor loser. That fall my broken heart healed as I hit newly harvested potatoes in a field with a bat, which Yaz did as a kid, and ate Yaz kielbasa on Big Yaz Special Fitness White Bread ("For youngsters of all ages"). The next year I gulped down Yaz's autobiography in two days. I was surprised by his nervousness during the final two games against the Twins. I was impressed by his friendship with his maternal grandfather, with whom he caught crabs, ate ice creams and watched movies. When I learned Yaz cried after learning that Grandpa Skonieczny had died after an operation, I cried, too. Yaz's airtight bond with his grandfather made me wish I had known my grandfathers, who died before I was born.

My sadness made my father even kinder. He consoled me by telling me stories of following the Philadelphia A's when they were ridiculously bad, after Manager-Owner Connie Mack sold Jimmie Foxx, Lefty Grove and other stars to pay the team's Depression debts. In 1934–1939 the A's lost 167 games more than they won, which made them 66 games worse than Yaz's 1961–1966 Red Sox. Dad received no consolation from his father, a Mennonite minister who dismissed baseball as a worldly waste of time.

Baseball became my ticket to my father's other worlds. He invited me to listen to his whimsical animal poems and harmonize with him on Sinatra saloon tunes. As he changed from Dad to Daddy-O, I moved from his shadow to his spotlight. Becoming his buddy, his fun catcher, was, without a doubt, the biggest miracle in the Year of Yaz.

Yaz's magic lasted only one season. In 1968 the Sox finished third, dropping from Cinderella, the queen of the ball, to Cinderella, the family maid. Lonborg won only six games after ruining a knee during a skiing accident. Scott's average plummeted to .171. Yaz hit 21 fewer home runs, drove in 47 fewer runs and dropped 25 points in average—partly because he tried to hit homers to rally a slumping team. He stuffed cotton balls in his ears to muffle boos from Fenway fans; at one point he taunted their razzing by melodramatically removing the cotton and raising his cap in a mock salute. Still, he won his third batting title, sparing the American League the embarrassment of a year without a full-time .300 hitter.

A few weeks after the season my father and I were again parked outside the Yastrzemski home on School Street, this time watching Carl Sr. rake leaves. We introduced ourselves, talked baseball for half an hour and entered the house to meet his wife and Carl's mother, Hedwig, or Hettie. Over coffee and pie my father gave me the best gift of all: he invited Yaz's parents to dinner at our home.

My mother treated the meal as a State Department banquet. She bought white china from Hildreth's in Southampton, one of the East End's best home-furnishings stores. She served ham because, after all, all Polish people love ham. While she chitchatted with Hettie Yastrzemski, Dad and I picked Carl Sr.'s brain. The elder Yaz enjoyed telling us that he outhit his son at age 41 on a semi-pro team in 1958, the last year they played together and the year I was born. He really enjoyed playing hardball with Sox executives until they signed Yaz Jr. to a $108,000 contract—plus two years of minor-league salary and college expenses. He relished raising his new bonus baby's weekly allowance from $5 to a whopping $7.50. "Didn't want him to get a swelled head," said Carl Sr., his deeply lined, leathery face cracking into a grin.

The Yastrzemskis left me with two presents autographed by their son. Within the week I lost the ball in the Wainscott woods. The photo is over my shoulder as I type. It shares a shelf with a picture of my father in a baseball uniform—also in his 20s, also smiling, also ready for life's 3–2 sliders. The pictures remind me of the magical year Yaz became my role model, Dad became my hero and both became my battery mates.

# (Anti-)Heroes

Truman Capote records the narration for the 1966 television version of his short story "A Christmas Memory," which made him the author's first literary hero. *(AP Images)*

# TRUMAN

My parents are attending an auction in Water Mill, hunting for cheap furnishings for the house they can almost afford. Mom is bidding on a small primitive painting of a young girl, something she loves but hardly needs. When she signals $300, Dad slumps and grimaces. He can't believe his normally frugal wife is willing to waste a mortgage payment on a useless decoration.

Mom is competing against a most extraordinary man. He has the squat build of a bulldog, the fey gestures of a matron in drag, the fashion sense of a peacock with spray-painted feathers. He wears a Panama hat, a floral shirt, shorts, long socks and windshield-sized sunglasses—a pretty gaudy getup for a summer morning among the linen-and-khaki crowd. Amusingly grotesque, he could be a friend of Uncle Fester of the Addams Family, my favorite TV clan. Charmingly gnomish, he could be the uncle, or aunt, of the girl in the picture.

The strange-looking stranger wins the painting at $325, then does something strange. He sashays over to Mom, bows, and kisses her right hand. "Madam," he says in a squeaky, lip-smacking voice, "you were a most worthy adversary."

Truman Capote—famous writer, infamous celebrity, Sagaponack's most renowned resident—admires my mother's feistiness. She blushes at his courtly praise. It will take her a few days to realize she was way, way out of her league at the auction. She could never, ever have trumped the deep-pocketed author of *In Cold Blood*—not in this lifetime or the next or the one after that.

Welcome to my first meeting with Truman Capote, my first favorite writer. He became my first favorite writer in 1965, when I was mesmerized by "A Christmas Memory," a short story shaped by warm memories of his chilly childhood in rural Alabama. I was seven, the perfect age to befriend Capote's alter ego, Buddy, a seven-year-old boy who makes merriment with his best friend, Sook, a mentally challenged cousin who acts much younger than her 60s. The pals gather pecans in a baby buggy so Sook can make fruitcakes for President Roosevelt and other worthy strangers. They run a museum with a dime admission and one sideshow: a three-legged chicken. They do these things to feel charitable, spiritually rich and, well, eventful.

To me, Sook and Buddy lived on another planet, where breakfast was fried squirrel. Yet, as odd as they were, they were oddly familiar, even familial. They made Christmas ornaments from the tin foil for Hershey bars. Well, my mother made Christmas ornaments from the lids for cans of frozen orange juice. Sook bought a Christmas tree two times taller than Buddy to stop the boy from stealing the star on top. Hell, I understood his mischief because holidays spanked the devil from me, too. I was five when I opened all my family's Christmas gifts, raced up to my parents' bedroom, and proudly showed them my toaster from Santa. Such heresy couldn't go unpunished, of course, and the next Christmas day the flu flattened me but good.

"A Christmas Memory" was the first story that made me feel at home among written words—under covers between covers. Never before had I actually shivered at lyrical expressions and lovely deeds. I tingled at buggy wheels wobbling "like a drunkard's legs," a terrier staring at a gift-wrapped bone on the tree "in a trance of greed." I choked up at Sook and Buddy buying each other kites, the only gifts they could afford, and flying them in a wind she called "the Lord's breath and wish." Even before I learned they would never again celebrate Christmas together, I sensed it in Sook's last words: "As for me, I could leave the world with today in my eyes."

My love affair with "A Christmas Memory" grew when I saw the 1966 television version narrated by Capote. My passion intensified the next year, when I met Capote under that auction tent, acting like a circus act. From that point I vowed to track him with Buddy-like curiosity; from that point the South Fork became Capoteville.

Actually, the South Fork was already Capoteville. Easily the East End's most visible celebrity, Capote seemed to pop up everywhere. I saw him at Guild Hall in East Hampton, the general store in Sagaponack, the post office in Bridgehampton. The one place I didn't see him was the place he loved the best. Several times each summer I parked my bicycle outside his compound in Sagaponack, which hid behind a wall of pines and privet. He bought the property in 1964 at the bidding of his companion, Jack Dunphy, a novelist and a dancing cowboy in the original Broadway production of "Oklahoma!" Capote had wanted to purchase an elegant weekend home in Westchester County to be near Bennett Cerf, his friend and publisher. Dunphy laid down the law, demanding that Capote buy a more rural, relaxing retreat a bike ride from saltwater. To please Dunphy, Capote acquired a small house on a six-acre parcel on Daniel's Lane, a bird sanctuary with a stunning view of one of the South Fork's best beaches.

Mr. Capote wears the sort of fetching hat and sly look he wore when the author first met him during a 1967 auction. *(Photofest, Inc.)*

A high hedge blocked most of the property; the only thing I could see from Daniel's Lane was a roofline. As with Norman Jaffe's house for Harold Becker, which was less than a mile southeast on Town Line Road, I was too timid to wander up the dirt lane and call on Capote. As with the Becker House, I had to wait for a magazine tour.

The spread in the January/February 1976 issue of *Architectural Digest* was both pleasing and puzzling. The exterior of Capote's house was strangely simple and primitive. Why, I wondered, would such a rich, refined writer live in a flat-roofed, barn-sided box? Even with a screened porch and a cathedral window, the building resembled a glorified shack. The interior, however, was delightful: airy, cozy, quirky. The living room featured two-story bookshelves reached by a rolling ladder. The floor was painted a shiny blue, a tribute to, and symbolic tributary of, the nearby sea. Capote particularly liked the floor at night, when it floated "like a big blue-green lake." He spread the lake effect by having wicker chairs and a spiral staircase covered in the same marine hue.

Always the outrageous egotist, Capote designated himself an architectural designer. Always the inventive linguist, he called the house's studded siding a "raincoat," the décor "run-down comfort." In a photograph he looked run-down comfortable, sitting in a well-worn chair by the fireplace, legs crossed, left hand pressed to chin and cheek, blue eyes chiming with blue bathrobe—a shabby-chic squire.

Capote considered the house less a residence than a retreat. Here he could peacefully read, write and think about writing. Here he could escape the pressures of fame as well as the pressures of the Hamptons party circuit, which, he insisted, ruined authors with weaker wills. "This is a place," he said, "to be alone."

For Dunphy, the place was too small for two writers. So Capote bought his life partner his own retreat 75 yards away. The nearness of the cedar-shingled cottage, which looked far nicer than Capote's glorified shack, enabled Capote, who wasn't much of a cook, to stroll over to Dunphy's home for hamburgers and potato salad. Dunphy took advantage of the close proximity, too. On January 29, 1966 he celebrated the publication of "In Cold Blood" the book after six grueling years by walking 75 yards and tacking a blessing on Capote's screen door: "Le Beau Jour (The Good Day)."

Capote loved the level, lushly lit South Fork, which he dubbed "Kansas with a sea breeze." As a Sagaponack host, he could be as elusive as a sea breeze. He instructed people who drove him home to stop on Daniel's Lane before they turned into his dirt lane. He wanted to save their cars from being scratched by shaggy trees along the driveway; he also needed the exercise of a short walk. Guests were generally discouraged from sleeping over, which he found "interrupting." Among the few friends allowed to stay the night was Lee Radziwill, who acted in a 1967 TV version of the movie "Laura" written by Capote.

According to a friend of both men, it was Dunphy, not Capote, who was truly, blissfully at home on the South Fork. "I didn't like Truman's house that much," says Tinka Topping, a retired psychiatric social worker who owns a horse farm in Sagaponack, also on Daniel's Lane. "It had slightly too much stuff, too much junk. Jack's house was pristine; his sense of simplicity and minimalism was more to my taste. I guess Truman liked the peace and solitude out here. Jack really loved it out here, much more than Truman. I don't remember Truman spending much time here in the winter. Maybe it was because his place was not winterized. Jack used to stay much longer. I never saw Truman on the beach whereas Jack was always picking up pebbles and driftwood."

Topping socialized far more often with Capote because he was far more social than Dunphy, whose devotion to privacy made him an honorary monk. She recalls the day in 1966 when Capote came to her horse farm to breathlessly announce his plan to throw a party to end all parties. Desperately in need of fun after *In Cold Blood*, he declared he was going to toast his friend Katharine Graham, publisher of *The Washington Post*, at the Plaza Hotel in Manhattan. Everyone, he said, would be required to wear black-and-white outfits and masks.

"I remember Truman coming to visit us—unannounced, like he always did—and saying: 'Listen, I have the best idea. I'm going to have a party and it's going to be famous,'" says Topping. "And everybody was going to be invited, from the plumber to the president. 'And no one will ever forget it.'

"I just couldn't believe that he would say that. So I said: 'Well, why is it going to be so special?'

"'Well, it's going to be at the Plaza. And it's going to be for Kay Graham'—back then you had to throw a party for *someone*. 'And you're going to have to come with Bud'—that was my husband.

"'But Truman,'" I said, 'I don't have a black dress to wear.'

"'You do just what I say. You go to Bergdorf Goodman [the deluxe department store in Manhattan] and you get yourself a plain black pajama dress.'

"So I got a black jumpsuit with feathers on it. And that's just what I wore. And it was a great party. And no one ever forgot it."

Capote's ball was, indeed, a ball. Andy Warhol arrived without a mask. Norman Mailer wore a trench coat. The host ordered an insulting gate crasher to leave the premises—*waltzing*. Not everyone at the ball, however, had a ball. The excessive preening of many of the 500-odd guests disturbed writer Edward Albee, who demolishes excessive preening in his play "Who's Afraid of Virginia Woolf?" Even before the Plaza extravaganza, "Truman and I spent very little time together—maybe two or three parties," says Albee, who bought property in Montauk in 1962, two years before Capote did the same in Sagaponack. "I stayed mainly in Montauk while he kept to his entourage around Bridgehampton. The ball sort of ended it for me with him. I didn't need to see him anymore. Truman became a celebrity—to his disadvantage. Celebrity is a lower form of life. It makes people feel satisfied because they can meet the writer never having read the work."

It was on the South Fork that Capote used his celebrity for charity. In 1966, his most epic year, he hatched a novel plan to help Topping raise money to open the Hampton Day School, a private academy in Bridgehampton. One day he told her that *Family Circle* magazine had promised him he could write an article about anything he wanted. He suggested she write the story under his name and then donate the fee to her pet project. Topping fully expected that Capote would change her Capote-esque copy inside out and upside down. "To my great shock, he left it alone, and we made $5,000," she says. "Truman gave validity to this little school in a big magazine. And he really couldn't have cared less."

Several years later Capote was invited to write a foreword to a book by Sag Harbor resident Myrna Davis about the lure and lore of potatoes, a South Fork bumper crop. Again, he asked Topping to be a ghostly ghost writer. This time she asked someone else to play literary ventriloquist. The anonymous author, another Daniel's Lane neighbor, slipped on Capote's purple prose like purple silk slippers. She described him preparing "an exhilarating country lunch" of small potatoes gleaned from a nearby field, baked, heaped with caviar ("which I have forgotten to tell you is the only way *I* can bear to eat a potato") and washed down with vodka ("*always* chilled, 80 proof and Russian"). The mini-essay ended, not surprisingly, with a plug for the Hampton Day School, "as open in spirit as its surroundings."

"I can't tell you the author's name: I promised to keep her identity a secret," says Topping with a chuckle. "Truman signed his name and when we sold the book at a benefit for the school, he sat and wrote his signature—this time for real.

"Depending on Truman's mood, you'd be glad he was around, or not," adds Topping. "I was very, very fond of him. I saw a side of him that many people didn't. I saw a much more gutsy, generous-hearted and incredibly smart and talented guy. A laid-back, real person. He was a great dancer too: he had a lot of rhythm."

Topping's farm was one of several South Fork stations where Capote sought solace. He swam at the Southampton estate of Gloria Vanderbilt, a model for Holly Golightly, the ingeniously ingenu-ous high-society escort in his 1958 novella "Breakfast at Tiffany's." He took a dip whether she was there or not, making him kin to the troubled suburban pool hopper in John Cheever's story "The Swimmer." He swam, drank and gossiped at the Sagaponack home of novelist Kurt Vonnegut, a member of a loose authors' guild on Sagg Main Street that included James Jones, Peter Matthiessen and George Plimpton. Capote was carrying on one day when he abused the ears of Vonnegut's neighbor, contemporary artist Robert Dash, who was gardening near their adjoining properties.

"I heard this incredibly querulous, repetitive voice coming through the hedges, with very little variation in its rhythm or tonal zone," says Dash, who over 40 years has transformed his two acres into the Madoo Conservancy, an encyclopedic, innovative series of gardens on the National Register of Historic Places. "It was just this childish prattle, and it gave me a headache. I thought it was a maiden aunt of Kurt's telling a story. And I thought, oh, how nice—that must be how Kurt became a storyteller."

Dash's wit is drier than the driest martini. Asked for the year of his Capote hearing, he quips: "Some time after the Boer War." He confesses he could have used a double martini and a Valium chaser to survive a Sagaponack lunch starring Capote, Capote's bulldog Maggie and Diana Vreeland, the fabled fashion editor and fashionista. "The repartee between Diana and Truman was like that of an old couple," says Dash. "She insisted her birchwood cigarette case was made by Faberge and he declared that, surely, it wasn't. They were talking about a mutual friend who had cracked up a car in Antibes and Truman said: 'Well, how is the car?' I mean, really. Truman was very spoiled, like a piece of cheese or a piece of ham.

"At one point I said: 'Mr. Capote, your dog is vomiting on my left sneaker.' He said: 'Oh no, she couldn't have done that.' And I said: 'You're right—she's doing it on my right sneaker.'"

A missing Maggie had a paw in a nicer Sagaponack story. On Labor Day 1974 Capote asked a man on Gibson Beach if he had seen "a little bulldog around here." Myron Clement, co-owner of a public-relations company in Manhattan, immediately recognized the fey gestures and the mincing voice. His reply was quick and Capote-esque: "No, Mr. Capote, but if you have a message, I'd be glad to deliver it."

The next day Clement met Capote again in, of all places, a fancy French restaurant in Manhattan. The coincidence and the quip, both within 24 hours, started one of Capote's truest friendships. Over the next decade Clement and his business-and-life partner, Joseph Petrocik, served as Capote's chauffeurs and companions, counselors and caretakers. Petrocik estimates that he and Clement drove Capote from Manhattan, where he kept a plush apartment, to the South Fork at least 100 times. Several times he stayed at their house in Sag Harbor because the living-room floor in his house in Sagaponack was still wet with marine-blue paint.

Petrocik and Clement tried to calm Capote during his stormy romance with John O'Shea, a native Long Islander, married father and bank executive who became the writer's manager and writing protégé. They grew accustomed to Capote's creative takes on reality ("He could really pirouette around a fact," says Petrocik) and homosexuality (He hated the word "gay," replacing it with "yag," which sounds like a kid's mispronunciation of Jaguar). They witnessed his terrible parking and experienced his horrible driving of his Buick Riviera, a cabin cruiser of a car. Capote could be distracted by his dog hanging out a window, threatening to become a canine trapeze act. Or he could be impaired by a toxic cocktail of alcohol and anxiety. Or he could be handicapped by poor eyesight and low height. After all, at 5-foot-3 he barely cleared the top of the steering wheel.

Another story about Capote's driving is kinder and gentler. It comes from writer A. E. Hotchner, the memoirist ("King of the Hill") and biographer ("Papa Hemingway") who built with his dear friend Paul Newman a philanthropic empire built on salad dressing, popcorn and other dietary staples. One summer Hotchner rented a home on Town Line Road in Wainscott, near Capote's compound in Sagaponack, and shared a gentle game of literary gamesmanship. Most days that summer, usually around 1 p.m., Capote would motor by Hotchner's place in the behemoth Buick and yell: "Hotch—are you there?"

"Yes, Truman, I'm here."

"Are you working?"

"Oh no, Truman."

"Oh good!"

The encounter with Hotchner shows that Capote liked to compete even when he was supposed to be retreating. In 1969 he found a public place on the South Fork where he could show off, casually. That year he began frequenting Bobby Van's, a Bridgehampton bar-restaurant named for its owner, a pianist who played mean Gershwin and Porter. Capote cultivated an oasis among the paneled booths, Tiffany-style lamps and diverse patrons. He made the saloon a salon for dishing about scandalous socialites, bitchy models and wrecked writers.

Van and his wife, Marina, doted on Capote, celebrating his birthday in a newspaper ad, giving him a forum and a second home. "To us, he was not a celebrity; he was just Truman coming in to have lunch," says Marina Van, executive director of the East Hampton Chamber of Commerce and an authority on South Fork author-drinkers. "I know he was comfortable in our place. Afternoon conversations with him were fun, interesting, filled with laughter—the feeling you would get talking to a college roommate."

Some Bobby Van's customers were less collegial. They were annoyed by Capote's loud, drunken antics and drunken, louder exits. These sordid scenes, part of what Tinka Topping calls "Truman's all-flimflam side," spoiled all sorts of professional and personal partnerships.

Capote, for example, sabotaged a working friendship with Eleanor Perry, a successful screenwriter who summered in Amagansett and Wainscott. In 1966 the pair adapted "A Christmas Memory" for TV with director Frank Perry, Eleanor's husband. The trio got along so well, Capote invited the Perrys to his Black & White Ball. Yet, according to Eleanor's son, crime novelist William Bayer, the union began fraying the same year, after she and Capote won an Emmy Award for their "Christmas Memory" script.

"As they left the dinner and the paparazzi crowded round, T elbowed Eleanor aside while placing his arm around his 'date,' Lee Radziwill, as he faced the cameras," says Bayer in an e-mail. "And of course, from his POV, this was a smart move, as Ms. R. was Somebody to be seen with, and Eleanor Perry was . . . well . . . nobody. I don't think my mother ever forgave him for that move."

Eleanor forgave Capote enough for a second and a third collaboration. In 1969 she and Frank Perry produced "Trilogy," a film of three TV versions of Capote stories, including "A Christmas Memory." The same year Guild Hall in East Hampton screened "Last Summer," the Perrys' movie about four teens sharing social and sexual adventures on Fire Island, as yet another benefit for the Hampton Day School. Capote appeared in a promotional photo in *The East Hampton Star* looking weirdly subdued, seemingly moonlighting on Planet Normal.

It took Eleanor Perry another decade to settle the score. In 1979 she skewered Capote in the novel *Blue Pages*, a bitter satire of her screenwriting experiences. The same year Capote expressed his dissatisfaction by shunning Perry in the green room of a Chicago talk show. "There was, shall I put it," says Bayer, "a certain frigid acknowledgment."

Bayer recalls one other sad episode, this time involving Frank Perry. Divorced from Eleanor, he was in Capote's home when the latter pointed to a box of paper on a desk. "There 'It' is!" Capote shouted. "It," he intimated, was *Answered Prayers*, his much-publicized, often-postponed, ultimately unfinished novel of thinly veiled, revengeful portraits of Gloria Vanderbilt, Tennessee Williams and other famous former friends. According to Bayer, Perry looked in the box and saw nothing but blank pages.

Ambushed by booze, cocaine and anger, Capote joined the company of his scary Southern Gothic characters. His reading at Town Hall in Manhattan, organized by Topping as a Hampton Day School fundraiser, was a stumbling, fumbling disaster. He slammed his Jaguar XKE into a Bridgehampton tree early one Sunday morning; the same day he was visited in Southampton Hospital by the Rev. Bob Battles, my minister at the Bridgehampton Presbyterian Church. Jailed in Southampton for drunk driving, he passed the time by signing copies of his books for friends of the sheriff's wife.

After leaving the slammer, Capote appeared in a Southampton court wearing garish shorts. He thought the judge would find his apparel charming and let him off the hook for the DWI charge. Instead, his driver's license was revoked and his poor etiquette scolded by Justice Mercator Kendrick, a name that could have been conjured by Capote.

Despite these offenses, I fondly remember Capote as a kind of magical absentee uncle. More than 40 years after he sucked me into "A Christmas Memory," he remains the life poet who made me realize that words can do fantastic tricks. The sneaky sociologist who made me see Holly Golightly in my father, a Mennonite minister's son who became a social bulldozer on Madison Avenue. The snake charmer who made my mother feel as special as Miss Golightly, just because she failed to outbid him with fierce flair.

# JAKE

I'm shooting hoops at The Forum, flinching every time the ball springs from the rut under the backboard into Jake Murray's rhododendrons. I'm in the rhodie den, trying to ignore yet another broken branch, when Jake shuffles across the circular driveway by his modular house-studio. His hair is tangled, his shoulders are slumped, and he's scowling. Something tells me he's going to give me holy hell for screwing with his shrubbery.

Instead, Jake gives me a gift: the March 1968 edition of *Playboy*, the one with an interview with Truman Capote, my favorite writer. Jake, who's training me to be an author, thinks it's high time I read Capote on Capote, even though he thinks Capote is an "over-rated twerp."

Before I can thank him Jake grabs the *Playboy* from my hands. "You oughta see Miss March—great big tits," he says gruffly, the way he gets when his brain is rattled by too many messages. Then he shakes open the centerfold to bare Michelle Hamilton's bodacious ta-tas for me and anyone else passing by on Foxcroft Lane. And then he flashes a grin so disarmingly charming, why, it would make the devil walk on water.

Every boy needs someone—preferably, someone outside the family—to get him straight through life's crooked narrows. My guy was John F. Murray Jr.—copywriter, novelist, journalist, writing mentor, sex coach, married bachelor, alcoholic, manic depressive, bipolar role model.

I was first drawn to Jake by his house, the Westwoods' jauntiest joint. The one-story, two-bedroom, flat-roofed, white-and-gray wooden rectangle was a kind of sophisticated cabana, the only place in the neighborhood that really belonged at the beach. The décor was pure sixties swinger, anchored by a black-leather Eames lounge chair, an orange sofa and a free-standing Danish-modern stove. Indeed, Jake's place was less a home than a writing lair, a working retreat from the shingled New England cottage next door that he shared with his second wife, artist Marie "Mimi" Harriman, and their broods of children. Even though the studio was built for Mimi to share, it was no woman's land. Surely, a grown, sane female would have never let crumpled papers pile around the typewriter like sagebrush, or permitted cigarettes in the refrigerator.

The shrine at Jake's joint was a row of four seats from Ebbets Field, the late home of the late Brooklyn Dodgers, the baseball team that brought him great joy and greater sorrow. Mike Raffel and I sat in those creaky thrones while skimming *Playboys*, sipping bottled Pepsis and listening to Jake treasure the Dodgers as a hometown tribe. Being young and impressionable, we were naturally impressed by Jake's tales of a rare era when players were known by their first names (Jackie, Pee Wee) and nicknames (The Duke, The Barber); when players and fans lived in the same apartment complexes; when whites and blacks sat next to each other rooting for "Da Bums" and supporting their crazy supporters (the ragtag Sym-phony Band, Hilda the cowbell clanger); when Brooklynites of all stripes were united by hatred for the cross-town, ultra-successful, goddamned uppity New York Yankees, who defeated the Dodgers in five World Series from 1941 to 1953. When the Dodgers finally beat the Yanks in the 1955 Series, it was much more than underdog becoming top dog. It was, Jake said, "like visiting heaven for a day, pissing at St. Peter's Gate, and not getting a one-way ticket back to hell."

Jake's place was a heaven of hedonism. He let kids curse their parents, ask rude questions and generally misbehave without fear of punishment. One of the youngsters who prospered in this den of iniquity was his stepdaughter, Dorothy "Tiger" Borland Kitt, a child of Mimi's second marriage. "My father was nuts and my mother was strict, but with Jake I could get away with being a smart-ass," says Kitt, a social worker and psychoanalyst. "In my world, before I met Jake, children were considered a great point of humor, a fashion accessory. I never had a grown-up to count on, to get advice from, to bounce things off. And Jake was all that for me.

"He told spectacular stories about motorcycle accidents, sliding under a truck and suffering amnesia, to cover for the fact that he'd disappear, that he'd been in psychiatric hospitals. He'd take his green Volkswagen Bug and stick Irish flags in it and take me toy shopping in Southampton—whoopee! He taught me to swim. I could fuss over him; I got to make him nice dinners on Fridays. He was protective. I got to act out appropriate things on him as a father."

A conversation with Jake was always a seesaw. He might tell you he supported the legalization of pot—but not pot heads. He might put a lit cigarette in his ear for pure shock value, then denounce the Catholic church's original-sin platform as "a crock of shit."

"He looked down on me because I wasn't a ladies man," says Jake's son, Jeff (aka John F. Murray III), a long-distance trucker. "To him, I was a dateless wonder. He also gave me crap about my short hair, and not liking sports, and not smoking pot. It reminded me of that *New Yorker* cartoon with the hippie mother and father and the Boy Scout son and the caption: 'Where did we go wrong?'"

When Jake was happy, relatively sober and properly medicated, he resembled George Kennedy in "Cool Hand Luke." When he was unhappy, drunk and improperly medicated, he resembled Lee Marvin in "Cat Ballou." I could read his moods because he was basically a carbon copy of my father. Both were born in the early 1920s and grew up in large families led by prominent fathers. Both settled in the suburbs and worked in the advertising business in

Jake Murray, the author's first writing and sex coach, looks confident and peaceful in 1969, the year his novel *The Devil Walks on Water* was published. *(Photo courtesy of Matt Murray)*

Manhattan. Both enjoyed being burrs in the ass of complacency. Both had the infuriating habit of leaving arguments they started, retreating to the sideline to referee and judge. Both played tennis as a slicing, dicing blood sport. Both masked their manic depression with booze, Lithium and letters to their worried kids insisting they were fine when they weren't.

Like my father, Jake relished being a rogue. In reality, he was a card-carrying member of the Irish-American aristocracy. His grandfather Thomas Murray was a renowned inventor with nearly 1,100 patents, second in number to another Thomas—Edison. He developed everything from refrigeration systems to a boiler nick-named "The Murray Wall of Water." These devices made him rich enough to give his grandkids $100 gold pieces on their birthdays.

Jake's father John F. Murray, or Jack, was an electrical engineer who at age 11 invented a string-and-pulley baseball board game endorsed by none other than Thomas Edison. A savvy puller of political strings, he was selected commissioner of the Port Authority of New York by Gov. Franklin Delano Roosevelt. In 1930, a year after his father died, he paid $250,000 for a seat on the New York Stock Exchange. When stock prices plummeted, he raised his spirits by drinking Scotch from a medicine bottle in an Exchange bathroom.

Jake's mother Jeanne, a former model for society painter Howard Chandler Christy, married Jack Murray when she was 19 and carrying their first child. Every summer the couple escaped with Jake and their six other children from humid, oppressive Brooklyn to Lighthouse Farm, a 56-acre mini-estate on the Murray clan's compound in Southampton, a 160-acre wonderland for three families with 32 children. The compound was a paradise of fresh- and salt-water pools, cooks and chauffeurs, equestrian contests and celebrity guests. Actor-playboy Errol Flynn skinny-dipped in a pool so clogged with little Murrays that family friend Al Smith, a four-time New York governor, joked he was afraid to dive in for fear he "might swallow a baby."

The Murrays were loud, lively and larger than life, says Alison Gray, Jake's first wife and a Long Island native. "They had these great big conversations that turned into arguments and competitions around the dining table. They used to take virtually everything they owned to Southampton for the summer. They had an expression for it: 'How do we get the bicycles out in the spring?' We've always used that expression as the kind of worrying that never does anybody any good."

One of Jake's sisters insists he had a fairly cheerful childhood. "He was very popular; he always had lots of friends," says Patricia Wood, who lives in a converted chicken coop on the Murray compound in Southampton. "He was a terrific guy. Everybody adored him." Yet the adult Jake swore he was a boy black sheep. All the stories he told me about his youth were sacrilegious, intended to tarnish his clan's golden halo. According to him, the Southampton Beach Club, a snobby WASP enclave, offered a membership to his Catholic grandfather only to gain easier access to Thomas Murray's filtration system, which removed sand from the club's saltwater pool. Jake insisted that his father tired of a family priest who clocked him coming to Mass with a railroad watch and scolded him for being late and "bombed as a king." When the priest, who was tired of the Murrays spending more time in their private chapel than his, began damning Jack Murray from the altar, Jack would leave the church for a smoke with his fellow hung-over buddies. They dubbed themselves "the firemen."

Jack Murray balanced bad deeds with good. One time he bought new shoes for one of Jake's more unfortunate friends, a Southampton lad who attended Mass with the Murrays. "My father thought that by repairing the holes in the poor boy's soles, he could repair the holes in his soul," said Jake with a shrug and a smirk.

Jack Murray died in 1937, a casualty of a congenitally bad liver assaulted by buckets of booze. Buried the day before his 38th birthday, he joined a long line of tragic family victims. Members of Jack's generation suffered polio, Parkinson's disease and death by choking on a chicken bone. Members of Jake's generation were cursed, too. One married his sister's governess; another's mother hauled him into children's court for chronic expulsions from school. Three of Jake's sisters escaped the curse by marrying powerful men: a Vanderbilt, an Italian marquis and God (Constance Murray was a nun).

In the fifties and sixties Jake lived as a functional dysfunctional with his first wife and their three children in Weston, Conn. He was a copywriter who assisted the popular Texaco campaign "You can trust your car to the man who wears the Star." He attended A-list parties, including one at the home of William Styron, author of the best-selling novel *The Confessions of Nat Turner*. Jake's daughter, Melinda Murray McDougal, fondly remembers her father not only reading her Farmer Brown stories but illustrating them too.

"I adored my father in the fifties," says Jeff Murray, "before the breakdown."

This suburban idyll was spoiled by mental illness. Jake spent time in the mental ward of Bellevue Hospital in Manhattan, where fellow residents included poet Robert Lowell. Alison Gray says Jake became enraged by her "lewd" performance as Tessie Tura, the Texas Twirler, in a 1962 production of "Gypsy." That night her jealous husband tried to strangle her in her sleep. She was "in the very short count of dying" before Jake snapped out of his homicidal mania, told her to call the police, and spent the night in jail. For the next four years she kept a pair of scissors under her pillow.

Jake was "an injustice collector," says Gray, then a newspaper reporter and later an art teacher. "He knew about lust, but affection was not a word in his vocabulary. I mean, holding hands was something he did not understand. He could be full of charm when he wanted to be, and he could also be repulsive. I guess that could be said of many of us."

Gray and Jake separated in 1963 and divorced in 1966. Three years later he married Marie Harriman, the child of a bank owner, a debutante and a member of the Colonial Dames of America. Mimi was a bridesmaid at Jake's first marriage, a situation Gray calls "sort of Noel Coward."

Harriman was a petite beauty, a former model with beguiling eyes and cheekbones. "My mother drove men and women wild," says Kitt. "They all just had massive crushes on her." Yet she could be edgy, selfish and irresponsible enough to play strip poker with Jake in front of her daughter. "My mother belonged to that generation of WASPs who unraveled," says Kitt. "You know, you have money and looks and blah blah blah. My God, it was like the fall of the Roman Empire."

In 1969 Jake started his own empire. In addition to marrying Harriman, he published his first novel, *The Devil Walks on Water*, a satirical chronicle of the Murrays of Southampton set during the 1938 hurricane that wrecked the South Fork. The titular devil is Brian "Briney" Mitchel, the bad apple of a wealthy Irish-Catholic family, a composite of Jake and a cad of a cousin. Briney, a wrestler at Princeton, likes to drive his Ford Phaeton across pristine lawns and lick orange juice off women's nipples. He courts danger by bedding the wife of a motorcycle cop. He courts danger *and* heresy by chasing Millicent "Midge" Crocker, a Protestant whose father is a special agent for the FBI.

The hurricane sets in motion a Harold Lloyd comedy—that is, if Lloyd did pornos. Briney initially ignores the raging storm, his thoughts all wrapped up in a bodacious blowjob from an Irish maid. After erupting, he leaves "Peggy Something" on the bed ("a wonderful sloshing trampoline"), tries to escape on the roof, gets hit by a casement window opened by his sister and falls into the ocean, where he has a "wrestling match with this act of God called a hurricane."

From this point Briney becomes James Bond Jr. He takes refuge on the roof of Midge Crocker's house, which is swimming in Lake Agawam; opens it with axe and hands, and rides with Midge to safety on a plank. The finale is a mythic hoot: "From the shore they made a sight to behold, Ulysses and Venus on a surfboard in all their naked glory, bloody breasts and all."

*Devil* is a terrific beach read dosed with sneaky sociology— a splendid car crash between *The Great Gatsby* and *The Swimmer*. Jake exposes the dirtiest secrets of Irish-American aristocrats: anti-Semitism, homosexuality, paying Christmas bills with stock dividends, married couples sleeping apart in identical French

Provincial cottages. He uses the hurricane as cosmic revenge for such godless acts as building mansions on fragile dunes.

The novel made Jake the king of the Westwoods. He lorded it up by sticking a *Devil* bumper sticker on his AMC Pacer and having the title painted in yellow on the side of that green Volkswagen Bug. He publicized the book during East Hampton's July 4 parade and received greater publicity from a profile in *The East Hampton Star*. Perhaps his top tribute came from novelist and Sagaponack resident Kurt Vonnegut, who blurbed that *Devil* was the best blowjob in the history of class warfare.

*Devil* became my bible of sexual thrills. Sitting in one of Jake's Ebbets Field chairs, I memorized all the dirty scenes. My favorites were the epic blowjob, where the Irish maid found, "as she had found in the semen of Kerry, the salt and oil of the earth," and a watchman masturbating while imagining women in new two-piece bathing suits. Jerking off must have been sinful, because it was followed by the hurricane dismantling the little hand of a country-club clock—surely, a cosmic blowjob.

It was this combination of publicity and perversity that made me want to be a writer. Sensing my desire, Jake gave me my first writing tips. No. 1: Write what you know best. No. 2: Write what you want to read most. No. 3: Make a difference. No. 4: If you can't make a difference, at least make a racket. No. 5: And for fuck's sake, don't be a manic depressive—writing is bipolar enough without being bipolar.

Jake's good times went bad quickly. In December 1969 Mimi had surgery to remove a cancerous clot from her stomach. After losing

27 feet of necrotic intestine, her weight dropped to 75 pounds. On September 2, 1970, her daughter Nonnie's birthday, she died during an operation for diverticulitis. Jake scattered some of her ashes on the ocean and kept the rest in an urn in a bedroom closet.

Mimi's death shattered Jake's sanity. He abused booze and refused to take his Lithium, which Mimi had reminded him to take by leaving messages on the bathroom mirror. "I thought he died when she died," says Kitt. "He sat in the living room and screamed: 'I want her back! I want her back no matter what!' He just gave up and let things unravel. He used to say 'I have a goddamned freight train in my head.' "

It took a village to keep Jake's train on the tracks. His house was cleaned by Karen Raffel, Mike's sister. Some of his meals were cooked by Rosie Raffel, who was born the day of the 1938 hurricane. Laura Montant brought him cigarettes, groceries and other essentials. Mike and I kept him company.

We all knew that Jake couldn't live long without a female companion. In June 1971 he proved us right by marrying Frederica Bishop "Binky" Mason, a 1959 graduate of Sarah Lawrence College, another high-society school. Their union was tumultuous, partly because she was much younger, partly because Jake, says Kitt, "did not court women as much as he roped them." By March 1972 they were separated.

Jake found some satisfaction as a roving writer for *The East Hampton Star*. His periodic stories gave him the chance to indulge in humor, fantasy and self-promotion. He gave a copy of *The Devil Walks on Water* to Robert Moses, the master builder of highways, bridges and tunnels in metropolitan New York, during an interview about beach erosion. He revealed that he shared a shrink with

Irving Wallace, author of *The Chapman Report* and other best-selling novels. Jake "had an attraction to, if not the rich and famous, at least the creative and famous," says his daughter Melinda Murray McDougal. "Yet he rejected the trappings."

Jake made *The Star* a bully pulpit for humane treatment of the mentally ill. In one article he endorsed Sen. Thomas Eagleton, who dropped out as George McGovern's 1972 vice presidential running mate after being tarred and feathered for revealing he was treated for depression. Jake rejoiced that electroshock therapy, which he and Eagleton had received, "is finally out on Main Street where it belongs. It's often the chief topic of conversation—like a broken leg in a cast."

Jake's story helped me cope with my father's shock treatments. In fact, living with my father helped me understand Jake, while visiting Jake helped me live with Dad.

There was one time when Jake became a surrogate dad. In the fall of 1967 I was sitting in an Ebbets Field chair, perusing a *Playboy*, when he decided it was high time for my first sex lesson. "You know, if you want a girl to eat from your hand," he blurted, "you have to eat her."

"Eat her?" My virgin brain envisioned that Herb Albert and the Tijuana Brass album cover with the naked woman up to her nipples in whipped cream, coyly licking the white stuff from a come-hither finger, a sixties wet dream for so many hemi-hormoned boys.

"Eat her. Between her legs. Down *there*."

Despite the clues, I was still clueless. Recognizing my confusion, Jake drew a crude depiction of the female privates. "Lick her here," he said, pointing to the vaginal opening. "Suck her there," he said, pointing to the labia. "Nibble her up there," he said, pointing to the clitoris. "Do that, and I guarantee you she'll go wild. She'll give you a blowjob you'll never forget."

"Uh—what's a blowjob?"

Jake smiled, sighed and stared at me as if my head was my cock. "Let's save that one," he growled, "for another day."

# Sex, Booze & Barbershop

The Key Men, great singers and great friends. From left: bass Verne Behnke, baritone Bill Noble, lead Larry Gehman, tenor Gus Lopez. *(Photo courtesy of Bill Noble)*

# SEX

She was the first woman who gave me a hard-on and a heartache. She was a 29-year-old airline stewardess. I was a 9-year-old perv.

We met one weekend in 1967 at the house on Whitney Lane. She came with Verne Behnke, the bass in my father's barbershop quartet and an all-ages Romeo. She didn't care that he was 15 years older. I could tell by the way she rubbed her knee against his thigh under the dinner table.

She was va-va-voluptuous. Her breasts almost popped from her low-cut dress; I had never seen such ripe cleavage. Her hips humped the breeze. I drifted into a daze when she patted me on the butt with her fire-engine-red nails and said in a molasses-and-moss drawl: "You're so handsome, sugar!" For a few dizzying seconds I felt I was lying on the beach, eyes closed, ears tingling, thoughts circling like seagulls.

At the beach I watched men desire her and women envy her. When we returned home I went outside to watch her undress in the guest room. When she saw me I wanted to run but couldn't. She could have thrown a tantrum—or a stiletto shoe. Instead, she flashed a crooked smile and wagged a gentle finger. Her silent approval—"You're getting one free pass, but that's it, sugar"—produced my first live, one-on-one, bona fide boner.

The next day she gave me a goodbye gift. She kissed me on the ear, making it easier for her to whisper: "Hope you enjoyed yourself, sugar. Just don't make it a habit. A girl doesn't like being spied on." Her sexy secret left me with erection No. 2, which disappeared as she drove out of my life. Let me tell you, there's nothing like jealous sorrow to splinter a good woody.

An ocean resort is undeniably sexy. Beaches are crammed with arousing elements: tanned flesh, heaving breasts, swinging butts, sparkling water, warm sand, drowsy relaxation, heavy petting, heavier flirting. The South Fork in the late 1960s to early '70s was off-the-chart sexy. This was the era when many women switched from one-piece to two-piece bathing suits, flaunting their natural assets while leading the erotic-fashion revolution. Summer after summer the bikinis became skinnier, exposing larger areas of skin, exaggerating wiggles and aggravating jiggles. Summer after summer I stared longer and longer, which made it harder and harder to hide myself becoming harder and harder. Lying on a blanket I disguised my boner—which seemed as big and as obvious as a telephone pole—by turning on my stomach, shifting slowly to avoid breaking a blood vessel. Standing by the shore I jumped into the surf to freeze my frozen member.

Back then the East End just shimmered with sex. Amagansett had Asparagus Beach, named for the stalks of singles who at the crack of 4 p.m. stood up to signal they were free that night for a date and dessert. East Hampton had Two Mile Hollow Beach, a gay drive-in. Bridgehampton had the drive-in, where every third movie—"Romeo and Juliet," "Easy Rider," "I Love You, Alice B. Toklas"—showed young and middle-aged lovers in lust, sometimes with each other.

Wainscott had the gossip grapevine. Kids chattered about three-month romances between locals and summerites, with American-European dalliances earning the most chatter. Adults discussed John Updike's racy novel *Couples*, which kids read when their parents were away or asleep. I can't remember any parties where consenting adults went home for the night with the person whose key they plucked from a bowl. But I know my parents and their peers debated the repercussions of your spouse sleeping with your best friend's.

Fires were doused by killjoys trying to prevent the South Fork from becoming as free as the Riviera, as easy as Rio de Janeiro. In 1970 the Town of East Hampton banned the wearing of miniskirts in public in the Village of East Hampton. The puritans in power apparently worried that a lot of leg and a little underwear would cause too many accidents. Yet they refused to forbid hot pants, which were far more distracting and dangerous.

Municipal morality was looser on the Montauk Highway strip in Wainscott, the Town of East Hampton's Wild West. One of the

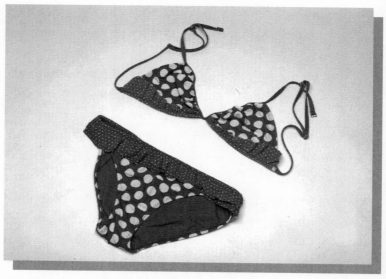

Tinier and tinier bikinis made South Fork beaches sexier and sexier. *(Photo by Chuck Zovko)*

most popular businesses was the Attic, a nightclub that catered to gay men. It shared a corridor with a motorcycle-mower dealership, an antiques store in a red barn and the Viking Diner, a fishermen's dive that advertised "sea going" coffee. Even as a kid I was tickled by the open-season zoning.

There was no zoning in *Playboy* magazine, my bible of healthy sexuality. Whether peeking at it in my house or lingering over it at Jake Murray's, I fell head over groin for women who seemed completely comfortable in their birthday suits. It wasn't just the photography and art direction that made them glow; they just radiated natural, neighborly eroticism. I was entranced by Liv Lindeland, the January 1971 Playmate, reclining on hip and elbows, golden hair snaking over a shoulder, an R-rated princess. I was excited by Marilyn Cole (January 1972), luxurious brown hair down to her nipples, standing against a bookcase with one leg up and rubbing against the other, an Amazon Emma Peel. Both Cole and Lindeland boiled my blood and steamed up the winter.

I was too young to fit *Playboy*'s bachelor demographics. I never wore a Nehru jacket, never bought skin-diving equipment, never drove a souped-up Javelin. I was old enough, however, to regard the magazine as a sexual forum. I was surprised by a story about homosexuality in the military. I was stunned by a pictorial on the film "De Sade" that featured actor Keir Dullea, who was so dull in "2001: A Space Odyssey," lapping strawberry jam from the breast of a delighted acolyte. My first sex academy was The Playboy Interview, where I learned about gay politics from poet Allen Ginsberg and swinging from quarterback Joe Namath. I also learned that Truman Capote was a literary drag queen who believed that at least 80 percent of prostitutes are lesbians.

Many people forget that back then *Playboy* guided women, too. Lesbians and straights, reactionaries and hedonists—they all endorsed editorials endorsing the right to use contraception and choose abortion. Even feminists who criticized the magazine as a glossy factory for brainless bunnies praised it for championing bra burning—although I'm sure they weren't as pleased about a pictorial on the no-bra look.

One of these *Playboy* fans was my first lover. I met Janellen in the summer of 1971 swimming in Georgica Pond. She was pale and blonde, tall and reedy, strangely curvy and muscular. She reminded me of a tomboy Connie Kreski, the January 1968 Playmate and another winter favorite. Janellen was, in fact, a tomboy who shared my passions for baseball and cars. Even better, she liked my curiosity. Better still, she loved my eyes, a huge turn-on for a 13-year-old turned on by pretty much everything, including the breeze.

For weeks we tested sexual boundaries—French kissing, caressing, groping below the Mason-Dixon Line. One afternoon at her house we crossed the border to serious fooling around. Janellen's parents were at a party, her sister was at a sleepover. After undressing in her bedroom, I decided it was time to practice Jake Murray's foolproof tips on oral sex. I began by circling my hands around Janellen's stomach. Encouraged by her moaning and twisting, I ran my tongue down the center of her body. When I stabbed her navel, she giggled. The second I licked her vulva she stiffened and pushed my head away with a palm.

"*What* are you *doing?*"

"Relax—you'll like it."

A pause. "Where did you learn this?"

"From a good friend. He even drew me a picture."

A longer pause. "Okay—as long as you know what you're doing."

"Trust me."

She did, and the great expedition continued. I nibbled and sucked; she wriggled and bucked. Her clit was between my lips when she shuddered and shouted. Jolting her pelvis in the air, she smacked my nose. We both laughed at the absurdity of painful pleasure.

We rested for what could have been six minutes or 69. I told Janellen about following Jake's instructions for the first time. She told me it was her first orgasm with a guy. Suddenly she smiled wickedly, rolled over and began drawing a line down the middle of my body with a tightly folded tongue. She zigzagged to my cock, which she kissed, licked and sucked with surprising dexterity. When I was about to come, she pulled her mouth off and yanked me to climax. It was my first mind-blowing, earthquaking ejaculation. What made it more thrilling was knowing she was watching, thrilled.

After my thoughts returned to my brain, I asked Janellen how the hell a respectable 13-year-old girl from a respectable family could be such a hellacious head hunter. She grinned, laughed and said: "I learned it all from The Playboy Advisor."

We toasted our success by drinking apple juice and eating strawberries. Lying leg over leg, everything popped. Curtains snapped. Waves sizzled. Car wheels transformed gravel into breakers smashing a jetty. The late afternoon sun turned Janellen's hair saffron. It seemed the world was making love to us.

That day I discovered the sensuality of sexuality. The best sex, I sensed, has nothing to do with staring at a Playmate or spying on a voluptuous stewardess. It's skin on skin, mind on mind, soul on soul.

# BOOZE

Mom, Meg and I are parked at the Bridgehampton railroad station for The Migration of the Weekend Dads. Every Friday night in the summer the train deposits dozens of fathers exhausted from working five days in Manhattan and riding two hours in a sweaty, rickety cattle car. Every Friday night my father arrives as loose as his tie, as wrinkled as his shirt. His eyes are bleary. His breath is a blast of gin and dry vermouth. He talks way too loud, as if to drown out the locomotive roaring in his head.

The four martinis he had that day are really doing the talking. That night he'll have two more with dinner. The next morning he'll play tennis with a buzz that somehow doesn't impair his game. That evening he'll have four more while partying with his tennis buddies. On Sunday he'll pickle himself for the long ride back with a couple of Bloody Marys.

On the South Fork boozing was as much a summer ritual as The Migration of the Weekend Dads. Manhattans allowed shy people to schmooze during the Georgica Association's season-opening and season-ending parties by the windmill. Beers enabled squares to square dance during the annual strawberry festival in the barn at the Osborn farm. Martinis helped my father forget the pressures of commuting from suburb to city to island, selling advertising space for underdog magazines, supporting three dependents and two houses. Drinking excessively also dulled the pain of a tense marriage made tenser by his excessive drinking.

Like many fun-loving alcoholics, Dad thought he was better on booze. Indeed, at certain times under certain circumstances, he

Favorite East End libations included Cutty Sark (for adults) and Manischewitz Concord Grape (for teens who thought they were adults). *(Photo by Chuck Zovko)*

was. Hepped up on gin and vermouth, his quips became quicker, his retorts tarter, his limericks lustier. You should have heard him turn "Bill Hogan's Goat," a ditty about a shirt-eating, train-flagging black sheep, into slapstick vaudeville. The spell began to shatter around the fifth martini or midnight, whichever came first. That's when Dad became a sloppy, angry bore; that's when his charmed guests stopped being charmed.

Actually, I discovered the annoying, strangely amusing addiction of alcohol not from my father but from one of his guests. The lesson began one summer weekend when Joyce and Pete Peterson, my parents' good friends, visited our Wainscott house. The Petersons were hardcore drinkers, which helped them handle their hardcore jobs as an oil-company lawyer and a publicist. They arrived armed with a half gallon of gin, the biggest container of booze ever witnessed by the Gehmans. The outrageous size fascinated my sister, who used her considerably impish wiles to con the Petersons into letting her carry the glass behemoth from lawn to house.

Of course, a half gallon of anything is usually too heavy for most six-year-olds to hold for a dozen steps. Sure enough, the bottle slipped from Meg's fingers. Unfortunately for her, and more unfortunately for the Petersons, it slipped onto a concrete porch.

The sound of smashing glass was both sickening and satisfying. It was so satisfying because it made Joyce Peterson so memorably sick. At first she stood stock still and stunned, as if Meg had dropped her six-year-old son, Seth, on his head. Then her gaunt body sagged and she seemed terminally ill, as if the gin was her last IV dripping away. Then she shuddered in grief and rage, the reflexes of a competitive drinker drained of her final advantage.

Just as shocking as Joyce's shock was her speechlessness. I had never heard her silent; I had never heard her not nattering away like some college-debate drama queen, ramped up on gin and cigarettes. For 10 seconds I truly thought she would fall to her knees and suck the evaporating elixir through a straw.

Too much hard alcohol caused a lot of unusual behavior, or misbehavior, in the Westwoods. Laura Montant, a beer fan, grew tired of attending neighborhood parties where beer wasn't served. So she took to bringing her own ale, which she carried while riding on the back of her husband Philippe's motorcycle. "I was very particular, very fussy," she says. "Of course, I was the laughing stock of the Wainscott gin-and-tonic-and-vodka crowd.

They thought I was quite a colorful sight, whipping around on a motorbike, holding my cold bottle of Schmidt's."

Hard liquor fueled one of Whitney Lane's most notorious parties, which took place across our lawn in and around a California rancher. That night many of the 100-odd guests drank gin-and-tonics and vodka from plastic cups. At one point my mother's best friend, Paddy Dickinson, fell and shattered a glass-topped coffee table, injuring her elegant English pride more than her body. At another point a snookered stranger pointed at Jane Kaufman and said: "There's no hope for you." Turning to my mother, he declared: "You—there's hope for you."

Youngsters shared drinking hijinks, too. High schoolers entertained themselves by spiking the sodas of junior high schoolers during the Georgica Association's beach bonfires. Ever the den mother, Rosie Raffel picked up smashed juveniles and ferried them safely to her house on Foxcroft Lane. "I wouldn't let them drive or even walk home, so I had them all over sleeping," she says. "I was forever bringing home a truckload of wacked-out kids."

Like many parents at the time, Rosie let her own children drink at home so they would be less likely to drink away from home. "We used to think it was okay because at least we knew where they were—at least we had some form of control," she says. "At least they weren't out drinking and driving. Because we drank, we didn't see anything wrong in it. But it was wrong thinking."

I drank away from home because my parents didn't let me drink at home. I followed my pal Mike Raffel to the Beach Lane Beach Bar—a pickup truck. There I gulped my first beers and guzzled Boone's Farm Strawberry Hill Wine straight from the bottle. I listened to trash talk and woozy promises to get the fuck out of Wainscott, the hick hamlet. The scene reminded me of the chorus of Don McLean's "American Pie," where "good ol' boys" sit in their Chevys at the levee "drinking whiskey and rye, singing 'This will be the day that I die.'"

Booze on the East End was the calm before the storm and the storm itself. For renters, it lengthened short summers. For residents, it shortened long winters made longer by emotional hangovers caused by the absence of renters. Whatever the season or reason, it ruined marriages, hopes and lives. I'll never forget the Sunday morning I passed a horrible car wreck on the Montauk Highway by Sagg Main Street. The fatal crash was caused by a drunk driver who treated the blinking yellow light as an invitation to accelerate.

In the early seventies concerned citizens founded South Fork chapters of Alcoholics Anonymous to prevent other wrecks. Meetings were held at the Wainscott Chapel and the Bridgehampton Presbyterian Church, our home sanctuary. According to the Rev. Robert Battles, Bridgehampton's liberal minister, donating space to alleviate alcoholism was just as much a spiritual civic duty as buying a New York Times ad to demand Richard Nixon's impeachment. "Opening up the church's parlors was worth it," he says, "even though it meant sometimes on a Sunday morning opening the doors to blow out the smoke."

My father never attended AA meetings in Bridgehampton or Wainscott. He was too stubborn, too vain, to discuss his drinking problem with strangers. Then again, I'm not sure he realized he had a drinking problem. He probably thought he was perfectly capable of keeping booze at bay.

Jake Murray, who had my father's mule-kicking streak, came to a few AA meetings in Wainscott, once smashing the chapel's chairs in a boozy rage. Relatives and friends believe regular attendance might have stopped him from trying to kill himself with a gun. Trembling from vodka and nerves, he missed the mark, merely grazing the side of his head with a bullet. When the vodka ran out he drove to a liquor store in Bridgehampton to buy more to give himself the guts to finish the job. The store manager called the cops to stop Jake, who didn't know, or didn't care, he was a bloody mess.

"I suppose my dad was a functioning alcoholic," says Jeff Murray. "But in those days to be a real alcoholic you had to be a street person."

Jake tried to wrestle his drinking demons with words. He wrote about watering holes in an insiders' guide to the Hamptons called "Sh!" He wrote first-person short stories starring an alter ego—an alcoholic, manic-depressive, woundingly clever Irish-American writer. O'Phelan orders a "double Russian vodka neat, like Capote" in a Massachusetts bar, then deduces the toothless maitre'd must have played hockey for the Boston Bruins. He criticizes his brother for forcing him into rehab, where he meets an AA leader. He verbally disembowels South Fork hypocrites: "On eastern Long Island, suicide is not punishable—not even unsuccessful suicide. In New York, you go to the loony bin; on eastern Long Island, you just get talked about."

One of my biggest Wainscott mysteries is why Jake and my father weren't drinking buddies. They could have shared so much about booze and sex and tennis and advertising and Lithium and class and righteous indignation. Yet I can't remember them together, even though Dad met his second wife through a couple who rented and bought Jake's cottage, even though Jake wrote about Dad's second marriage for *The East Hampton Star*.

Maybe they didn't want to hang out with a goddamned charming competitor. Maybe they couldn't face an evil twin in a cracked mirror. Maybe their train was just stuck at the station.

# BARBERSHOP

My sister and I want to strangle our father. We should be outdoors on this glorious Saturday, rummaging through the woods, rampaging through the waves. Instead, Dad is driving us from Wainscott to East Hampton on an errand, forcing us to learn the harmonies to, of all things, "Silver Bells." It's the wrong song, the wrong season, the wrong reason.

Dad drills us mercilessly. He sings the alto and tenor lines separately and slowly, then orders us to copy him note by painful note, syllable by bloody syllable. He becomes tougher as the harmonies become trickier in the echo phrases ("Hear them ring," "Ding-a-ling") and the tag line ("Soon it will be Christmas day"). He barks like a sergeant when we fumble the verse about city sidewalks "dressed in holiday style." Every mistake gets a scold ("Stay on pitch, goddamnit!"); every complaint gets a louder scold ("Quit griping!"). Dad is stuck in his "When you're ready to drop, drive on" groove, which makes the 1964 Impala a mobile prison.

On the trip back we somehow get it right: the bell-like tones; the sliding stroll; the snowflake sheen. Happy his kids have finally knuckled under, Dad changes from tyrant to proud papa. His eyes close, his eyebrows arch, his voice soars. As he conducts with one hand on the steering wheel, the car fills with his gleaming, grinning tenor. He's in evangelical ecstasy. And just like that, boot camp becomes church.

Nothing pleased my father more than harmonizing in a harmonious family. Singing was his pure Lithium, calming the crises of broken romances, financial mistakes and spiritual disappointments. Singing was his sanctuary, the only place he had perfect pitch.

Dad was seven when he learned that singing is nothing less than seductive selling. As an elementary schooler he traveled with his minister father from their home in Easton, Pa., to entertain and educate a mission in Jersey City, N.J. Rev. Gehman began meetings by steering homeless drunkards, faithless derelicts and other heathens to the proper path. Then my father sang cautionary hymns like "In the Garden" he learned from his mother, who played a mean white-gospel piano and set records selling the World Book Encyclopedia door to door. Impressed by Dad's high, sweet, remarkably poised voice, missionaries and heathens alike gave him nickels and dimes, a king's ransom for a Mennonite prince.

The Key Men rehearse in the acoustically dynamic living room of the Noble family home in the Georgica Association. From left: bass Verne Behnke, baritone Bill Noble, lead Larry Gehman, tenor Gus Lopez. *(Photo courtesy of Maggie Noble)*

Singing became my father's social and sexual lubricant. As a teen in Pennsylvania he used fundamentalist numbers to get under the skirts of fellow bible campers eager to be fondled by the handsome son of the all-powerful Elder Gehman. As a young adult in Manhattan he sang oratorios with the Collegiate Chorale, directed by Robert Shaw, the legendary conductor-arranger, and rock-of-ages anthems at Calvary Baptist Church, where he befriended a shy, shock-haired pianist named Van Cliburn. He courted lasses—including my mother—with Irish ballads and earned free drinks crooning Sinatra saloon tunes in bars like Bill's Gay Nineties.

Dad found his greatest pleasure in barbershop quartets. It took me a long time to understand why such a hip guy enjoyed the square tradition of joining three men in a cappella versions of corny valentines to wives, mothers and nineteenth-century virtues. Eventually I realized that barbershop suited a man with a big-city attitude and a small-town soul. The hedonist in him loved the ringing sevenths that, cracked just right, tingle head, chest and groin. The teammate loved the nimble vocal choreography—the seesawing rhythms, the rolling textures, the threading dynamics. The ham loved the melodramatic antics—the thrusting hands, the swinging shoulders, the mooning eyes. The athlete loved the fierce competitions. The salesman loved the showmanship. The lonely soul loved the comradery.

Dad performed in a half-dozen quartets. His favorite was the Key Men. They lasted the longest of his groups, from the middle 1950s to the early '70s. They traveled the most miles, from Quogue to Quebec City. They were adventurous, agreeable comrades who relished singing, talking, drinking, joking and draining life to the dregs.

Tenor Gus Lopez was the only child of a Puerto Rican father and a Swedish mother. A tri-boro fellow, he grew up in Queens, lived in Brooklyn and worked for a bank in Manhattan. He was skinny with dark eyes, a toothy smile and a slightly squeaky speaking voice; somehow he resembled a quieter, balder Desi Arnaz. His singing voice was reedy and floating, earthy and ethereal. He was the quartet's arranger because he had pitch pipes for ears. He often worked out parts at work, relieving the boredom of cashing checks. He also booked late dates at Masonic lodges, Elks clubs and other social halls.

Verne Behnke began singing barbershop in college, where he discovered there was a premium for natural-born basses. A native of Galesburg, Ill., he won quartet contests while studying at Princeton University. In 1953 a fellow Princeton graduate introduced him to my father during a beach volleyball game in Westhampton Beach, where Behnke and Dad rented homes with other bachelors. An advertising salesman for *American Girl* magazine and cable-television suppliers, Behnke had a broad, ruddy face; close-cropped, slightly kinky hair, and a jolly manner. His plush, lush singing penetrated concrete, stopped traffic and stirred the loins of many a lady.

Like my father, baritone Bill Noble first felt the stirring of singing as a child in church. Like my father, the Manhattan native sang pretty much everything: country hymns, glee-club tunes, operetta arias, children's ditties (they both adored "Bill Hogan's Goat"). A marketing official for a valve manufacturer, Noble had an easy smile, neatly parted hair, a back-slapping confidence and an Ivy League handsomeness; he could have impersonated actor Robert Culp in an Arrow Shirt ad. He filled musical gaps robustly and keenly, embracing his roles as the Key Men's chameleon and junk man. "All I had to do was find the missing note in the chord," he says, "and plug it in there."

My father sang lead because he had the neatest, truest voice. What separated him from most leads was his willingness to risk purity for perversity. He loved to push the peak of his range, bursting into almost operatic bouquets, daring himself to veer off key. It was part of his go-for-the-jugular personality, along with shocking strangers with rude comments and starting arguments for fun.

"Most leads sing flat at some time or another," says Behnke. "I can't remember Larry ever going flat. He was always on."

"You could sing as loud as you wanted with Larry and he wouldn't be thrown off," says Noble. "You have no idea what a pleasure it was to sing as loud as I wanted and never stick out."

The Key Men were a fraternity inside and outside the quartet. They frequently broke into songs during dinner parties at our house on Whitney Lane, picnics at Lopez's rented cottage in Hampton Bays by the Shinnecock Canal bridge and cookouts at Noble's home in the Georgica Association, which had an all-wood living room with dynamic acoustics. Behnke, the only bachelor, was a surrogate uncle to my sister and a lifesaver for my father, yanking him from bar brawls before bruises became broken bones and worse. Dad and Noble were close enough to be brothers. They bonded during their first meeting, a 1957 party in Manhattan when they sang scores of songs together. Noble was pleased and pissed that my father was a walking jukebox.

"Before I met Larry I said: 'Who's that sonofabitch who knows more songs than I do?' I think your dad knew 200 hymns by the time he was six. He used to say: 'Oh, the fifth verse goes like this.' He was uncanny. We used to have so much fun fooling around with hymns like 'Once to Every Man and Nation'—especially in the later verses. [Sings] 'By the light of burning martyrs,/Christ, thy bleeding feet we track'—Christ, isn't that a great visual? You could go through a book of hymns and Larry would know three-quarters of them. Your dad knew all the verses to everything he ever sang in his life. I used to be close to that, but he literally could drive me under the table he had such a memory. Christ, total recall."

Invariably their discussions about music became discussions about religion. Like my father, Noble came from a prominent church family. His paternal grandfather was a Methodist pastor who became a college president and, as executive secretary of the Juilliard Musical Foundation, traveled to Europe to hire most of the first teachers for the Juilliard School of Music. Like my father, Noble could quote biblical verses from memory and tell jokes that would make church ladies run for cover. His favorite statement about my father could have been a confession: "Gehman, you are the only person I know who is one part minister and one part whore."

"Your father and I came from similar tribes—that's why we got along so well," says Noble. "We grew up in that background of preach the gospel, spread the gospel. You know, when you've got missions to visit and sermons to preach, nothing gets in your way."

Both men considered singing a family calling and a form of personal salvation. "It's a Noble family joke that if you're born and you can't sing, they send you back," says Bill's daughter, Maggie. "I think my dad is only truly happy when he's singing. I've only seen him cry because of music."

No one in the Key Men was more passionate about music than my father. Dad was more than the quartet's lead; he was the key man. He managed, booked, recruited, coached, cajoled, badgered. He chose most of the numbers, saving money by picking public-domain tunes, rationalizing that most listeners "like the old songs better anyway." After he died I found among his papers a sheet filled with 65 suggestions. The list ranged from barbershop staples ("Let's Harmonize") to stardust standards ("My Funny Valentine"), spirituals ("Swing Low, Sweet Chariot") to pop hits (an Elvis Presley medley).

"Larry was the most competitive guy I knew," says Noble. "He never gave up; he was ferocious. He played squash with my cousin, who told me that Larry wasn't the most skillful player but he beat the most skillful players because he was so goddamned determined. The whole secret of his personality was: 'I'll play with you, and I'll play by the rules, but I'll whip your ass.'

"Oh my Lord, Larry knew a lot of ways to beat you," adds Noble. "His attitude with us was: 'Goddamnit, quit your griping, we can win this goddamn contest! His zealousness rubbed off on us. I don't know if we were a great quartet. But we were a damned good quartet."

My father took his most competitive field—advertising—and turned it into the Key Men's only original work, a moral satire called "The Peddler's Opera." Matching his own words to melodies by Stephen Foster and Gilbert & Sullivan, he charted the rise, fall and recovery of a cocky salesman named Johnny Winsocky. "I can crack your toughest buyer/I'm the guy you oughta hire," declares Winsocky during his job interview, borrowing the theme from the musical "Of Thee I Sing." Hired to improve sales in upstate New York ("he's socko in Skaneateles and a riot in Rochester"), Johnny spends more time drinking than pitching. He's in a bar, lamenting he'll be eulogized "as a monument to laziness and booze and pride," when an older, wiser salesman reads him the riot act. Johnny gets his act together and gets the soprano, an amply endowed secretary named Mrs. Titsworth.

"The Peddler's Opera" was Dad's musical scrapbook. He cut and pasted his fondness for patter songs, clever repartee and groaning jokes ("I see you went to Harvard," says Winsocky's future boss. "Oh well, I like a man who can overcome handicaps"). Winsocky was his stand-in, an exaggerated version of the salesman who spent 40 minutes schmoozing and five minutes peddling.

"The Peddler's Opera" was the Key Men's calling card. They performed it for the Whalers Chorus, a barbershop chapter in Sag Harbor headed by Donald Clause, a real-estate mogul and renowned vocal competition coach. My father used his business contacts to get gigs with the Sales Executive Club of New York and a Quebec City conference of million-dollar salesmen for Berkshire Insurance. The latter date was an over-morning sensation.

"We drove all day, had our last run-through maybe 10 minutes before we went on, then performed at the ungodly hour of 8 a.m. with no coffee or doughnuts," says Noble. "Forty-five minutes later, we were treated to a standing ovation; talk about motivational. It was a huge hit because your dad had called on most of those guys for sales meetings. I bet he knew 20 out of 100 of them by name. I tell you, Larry Gehman could talk anybody into anything."

"We laughed our asses off for three days straight," says Behnke. "The money didn't pay for the drive, but the laughter was priceless."

"Oh my Lord, did we laugh and sing up a storm," says Noble. "I never had so much fun in my life."

The Key Men remained friends after there was no Key Men. My father and Gus Lopez sang with Noble during the latter's second wedding reception. Behnke was a charter member of the Marcus Hook Hardware Company, a barbershop quartet Dad named after making a sales call in a gritty oil town in Pennsylvania. The pair also performed "In the Garden" at the Bridgehampton Presbyterian Church, where Dad soloed from time to time. With the minister away for the weekend, Dad and Behnke sang the hymn's rarely sung third verse, which instructs the lazy to leave the comfy garden for a fuller, livelier life. "We sang it loud and proud from the balcony," says Behnke, "giggling under our breath." My father giggled harder, tickled by the thought that theologian Reinhold Niebuhr declared "In the Garden" the dirtiest hymn of all time.

I enjoyed the Key Men's company more than I enjoyed their singing. For me, a rising rock 'n' roller, barbershop was hopelessly hokey. I couldn't stand the stylized harmonies and the antique accessories: the barber's arm garters, the frozen smiles, the beauty-pageant preening. I attended only one Whalers Chorus concert, and only because there was a magician on the bill. I resisted Dad's efforts to make me a barbershopper as strongly as I resisted his efforts to make me a salesman.

Yet barbershop got under my skin. As a kid I loved falling asleep to the Key Men singing during parties in our Wainscott house. Their easy, zesty sound cut through the floor of my bedroom like a buzzing lullaby. It was outside that bedroom, in fact, that barbershop entered my blood.

I was leaning against the chimney, straddling the peak of the roof. One ear was tuned to the crickets chirping in the woods; the other ear was tuned to an eight-track cassette of Crosby, Stills & Nash's first album, which they rehearsed at a house in Sag Harbor. Singing along with "Helplessly Hoping," I added my first original harmony and started sailing through the vocal slipstream with David, Stephen & Graham. Suddenly, I shuddered with delight. There it was: The Barbershop Tingle.

It was at that exact moment that my father's "Silver Bells" boot camp finally made sense. Harmony, Dad was trying to say, and sing, is all about filling holes, fitting in, belonging.

# The Turnaround Year(s)

The only known photo of the long-haired author in 1971–1972, when he lived full time in Wainscott. *(Photo courtesy of Mike Raffel)*

The Gehmans are riding the roller coaster known as the Old Montauk Highway. Dad is gleefully gunning the car at 60 mph, turning hills into ramps and the Impala into a flying gazelle. Meg screams with pleasure; Mom screams with displeasure. She's angry at her crazy husband, who is surely going to plunge us all off the cliff into the sea.

I'm inside and outside the commotion. I love the giddiness of sailing above the ocean without a boat. I like the slightly sickening feeling when my stomach jumps into my mouth. I don't like bashing my head on a metal ceiling. And I hate that this joy ride is slowly wrecking my parents' marriage. It reminds me yet again that the Gehmans are destined to travel in different cars.

My parents married each other for the right and wrong reasons. In 1957 they were attractive, energetic, reasonably responsible, frequently lonely and on the north side of their 30s. They wanted, or needed, children before they hit 40. They thought that together they could be good parents, maybe even good partners. Marrying a mere six weeks after meeting, they basically dodged each other's differences. Those differences became divisive after the arrival of kids; day-and-night parental methods made them greater strangers. Over 15 years they never found that comfortable middle ground between nature and nurture, safety and danger.

Their split widened on the South Fork, where we were happiest as a family. For Mom, the marriage began ending when Dad lost $10,000 of college tuition on a scheme to convert a Montauk windmill into a conference center. For Dad, the end came in a party game. During a dinner at the Kaufmans' house everyone was asked who they would save during a disaster—your spouse or your kids? Dad never really forgave Mom for choosing us over him.

For me, the end arrived in an accident. It was October 1970, and Dad and I were tossing a football in our New Rochelle home. As usual, he was throwing too hard at too short a distance, trying to sharpen my reflexes and toughen my hands. Accustomed to his training, I caught every pass but the one that cracked a window. Startled by the sound of breaking glass, Mom rushed into the den and yelled bloody murder. Tired of being scolded, Dad threatened to hit her, something he had never done. Too much gin and too little Lithium had made him a maniac, something I had never seen.

Mom, Meg and I ran across the street to safety at a friend's house. Dad was arrested and released under the care of his psychiatrist. Within the week he received electroshock treatment. For a few days he was lethargic, almost catatonic. It was a shocking fall for a high-wire acrobat.

After Dad recovered, he and Mom separated. By the summer of 1971 they realized they could no longer afford to run two houses. He gave her the option to live year-round in one home while he rented the other. She chose Wainscott mainly because it was two hours from New Rochelle, the source of most of her pain.

Moving to Wainscott made me ecstatic. Finally, I could spend four seasons in some of my favorite places with some of my favorite people. Eighth grade on Long Island, I figured, had to be better than seventh grade in Westchester County, where the transition from elementary school to middle school was pure misery. Even now, nearly 40 years later, I swear it rained every third day.

Our year in Wainscott had a strangely sunny start. My first bus trip to East Hampton Middle School was my first bus trip to school after eight years of being driven or walking to class. For the first time I traveled with kids outside my neighborhood. The first one I really noticed was Barbara Mason, who lived on Wainscott Hollow Road in a tar-roofed cottage-shack, by the potato fields her father helped farm. She was irresistibly cheery and sexy, petite and voluptuous. I dug her crazy Afro, too.

My instant crush on Barbara helped ease the nervousness of a first day in a new school in a new community. I calmed down when I sat down in homeroom next to another new transplant

A basketball game at the Forum, with Jake Murray's house-studio in the background. *(Photo courtesy of Mike Raffel)*

from metropolitan New York: Tom Green, a Manhattan native with a shy, sly smile and shoulder-length hair like mine. I thought we'd be picked on as hippie outsiders by our homeroom teacher, Robert Kibler, who had a military crew cut and a growling voice. His Marine gruffness turned out to be partly guff, and he quickly welcomed us into the fold.

Kibler was a science teacher and the assistant coach of the varsity football team, where I really began belonging. He and coach Bob Yardley, a social-studies teacher, managed the Bonackers to a decent 3–2 record. Playing organized football for the first time, I had a pretty good season as a 130-pound cornerback and tight end. I caught 15 passes, intercepted two, scored a touchdown on a 75-yard play and prevented six points by forcing a goal-line fumble. Slamming and evading people, I found out, was great therapy.

The second most memorable game that season came against Most Holy Family Catholic in East Hampton, Mike Raffel's school. That day I ran back three punts. Each time I was tackled by Mike, who held me to a pitiful 20 total yards because, of course, he knew all my moves. Each time he pinned me to the ground a little longer, giving himself more time to mash his victory in my face mask by saying: "You ain't goin' nowhere, Je-THRO BO-dine!" He won the battles; we won the war, 20–6.

The most memorable game came against William Floyd, up island in Mastic. Dad, making a rare family appearance that fall, watched me catch a 50-yard pass leaping between two defenders and return an interception 70 yards before being tackled on the one-yard line. He sat in the stands with Mom, Meg and a surprise guest: Gerhard Blume, a retired police officer and New Rochelle neighbor. The day before Mr. Blume had traveled more than five hours from Westchester to Manhattan to the Bridgehampton train station, quite a haul for a 78-year-old veteran of World War I. Not knowing our Wainscott phone number, he called Jane Kaufman, our Whitney Lane neighbor, who called my mom and asked: "Do you know a Mr. Blume?" He made the trip because he wanted to see me play football and because he was sweet on Mom.

My football success made a few girls sweet on me. Impressed by touchdowns and tackles, they looked past my bad acne and terrible fashion sense; this was the year I mismatched a pink-and-white floral shirt with blue-and-green-striped bellbottoms. Romance sizzled during slow dancing to the Moments' "Love on a Two-Way Street" and holding hands during three hours of "Gone with the Wind." Romance fizzled while dismissing accusations of backstabbing in a school stairwell, not exactly the best den for secrets.

It was a year full of firsts. For some unfathomable reason the East Hampton School District put me in a second-year Spanish class, even though I hadn't had a first-year class. The teacher pitied me by letting me sit silently in the back row for four months. He even looked the other way when I relieved my boredom by playing miniature football, scoring touchdowns by shuffleboarding a folded paper triangle until it hung over the edge of a desk, plucking extra points between goal-post fingers.

I bridged sports and socializing by joining a bridge class taught by my basketball coach, a jolly giant named John Ryan. I discovered a new passion for all my subjects, even wood shop. For the first time I made the honor roll. For the first time writing came naturally. More of a follower in the suburbs, in the country I became more of a leader.

My new confidence deepened my friendship with Mike, who was always confident. We spent more time hooping it up at The Forum, shoveling snow from the court for three-on-threes, beating bigger, beefier guys with traditional plays (pick-and-rolls) and tricky plays (bouncing the ball off the backboard as a pass). We spent more time listening to rock 'n' roll records: Jimi Hendrix's "Voodoo Chile," the Rolling Stones' "Ruby Tuesday," Mott the Hoople's "Violence." Our conversations matured from music to girls, sports to problems in our families. Supported by Mike, I felt like an insider among his pals; thanks to him, I never had to cross the great divide between locals and visitors. I may not have been accepted, but at least I was tolerated.

While I prospered, my family struggled. Meg felt out of place in fourth grade at Wainscott's one-room school. A natural hellion, she made life hell for her teacher, Edith Mansir, a fixture since 1944. Coaxed by her friend Michael Porter, who was even more of a hellion, Meg peeked up Mrs. Mansir's skirt to explore the rumor the teacher wore no underwear. Mrs. Mansir punished this infraction and other infractions by making my sister sit for inhumanely long stretches inside—not on top of—a wastepaper basket. The gulf between them widened whenever Meg left school to sing with my father in the chorus of the opera "La Boheme" at the Juilliard School of Music in Manhattan. Other teachers would have endorsed the project as a valuable extension course; to Mrs. Mansir, it was consensual hookey.

In defense of Mrs. Mansir, she had to dispense frontier justice because she was the only justice on the frontier. "She was strong willed and fiercely independent," says her granddaughter Susan

Helier, my eighth-grade classmate. "She had some serious opinions about education and children and the way they ought to be in the classroom. She could tell you anything about all her kids. She could remember them long after they left school. She just loved teaching."

Mrs. Mansir couldn't hold a rod to Wainscott's toughest teacher. Katherine Barnes, her predecessor, punished unruly small kids with a ruler and unruly big kids with a rubber hose.

Mrs. Mansir retired from Wainscott after the 1972 school year. We like to joke that Meg hastened her departure. The cosmic joke is that 12 years later Meg graduated from Mrs. Mansir's alma mater, the State University of New York's Brockport branch, and settled in Rochester, Mrs. Mansir's hometown. Today my sister is a middle-school counselor who tries to convince kids not to be as rowdy in the classroom as she was.

My mother had the toughest time on the South Fork. She felt lonely and lost apart from my father and her New Rochelle friends. She was comforted by Jane Kaufman and Jane's next-door neighbor, Margaret Demarest, a kind nurse who lived in an absolutely spotless contemporary Colonial. She comforted herself by playing bridge for the first time and volunteering at Southampton Hospital's new consignment shop.

Separated from Dad, Mom was courted by my old friend Jake Murray, who was separated from his third wife. She refused his advances, thinking he was "creepy." He persisted in typical Jake fashion, offering her six ladder-back dining-room chairs, a sort of date dowry. She threw him off her scent by accepting one, which she's promised to leave me when she leaves us all.

Mom never told me of Jake's propositions while we lived in Wainscott. She wanted to protect my friendship with my mentor, which was deteriorating due to his accelerating mental illness. In fact, she did a terrific job of hiding her troubles from me that year. She essentially freed me to feel more at home everywhere in my new year-round home: the Beach Lane beach; the fields where we gleaned small potatoes left after the fall harvest; the roof outside my bedroom where I screamed along with "Maggie May," "(I Know) I'm Losing You" and other songs from Rod Stewart's album "Every Picture Tells a Story."

By the spring of 1972 Wainscott had changed from a place to stay a while to a place to stay a long while. I couldn't wait to start ninth grade at East Hampton High School, where Mike and I would be football blood brothers. In nine months I had morphed from a summerite to a local-in-training, from a "them" to an "us."

That July I veered back to "them" a few miles from Disneyland. Mom, Meg and I were staying at my uncle's home in Anaheim, Calif., when Mom received a shocking telephone call from one of her bridge partners, a real-estate agent in East Hampton. Dad, she learned, had sold the Whitney Lane home without her permission. She hardly cared that he had made an on-paper profit of $35,000, an excellent return on a six-year investment. To her, it was the ultimate betrayal and the official end of their marriage.

Being evicted from Wainscott made me furious. I never knew I could be so pissed at anything or anyone. Dad, I felt, had yanked a magic carpet from under me and wrapped me in it, trapping me like a caterpillar in a textile cocoon. I prepared for returning to New Rochelle by listening over and over to "American Pie," a bittersweet anthem written by Don McLean, who grew up in New Rochelle. I felt better imagining myself as the narrator, a "lonely teenage broncin' buck" who careens through crisscrossing universes of dancing romantics and marching-band rebels, a crown-stealing jester and a satanic nightclub singer, Buddy Holly and the Byrds, Lenin & Marx, joy and sorrow and hope and hopelessness and a whole "generation lost in space."

After a few months I found my footing and lost most of my anger. Back in New Rochelle I made a few great friends and met a few good teachers, including my second writing coach. I forgave Dad, especially after he gave me a Wainscott reprieve. In 1974 he married Dorothy "Dolly" Reed, a sassy, smart Shirley MacLaine lookalike who owned an orange-sided, barn-like house on Beach Lane, one of my favorite Wainscott residences. The ceremony took place at Bridgehampton Presbyterian Church, where Dad was a tenor soloist, and was filmed for an NBC special on second marriages. Flashy lights and whirring cameras turned the event into a carnival, blackening my already gray mood. I left the reception at the Beach Lane home early, without telling anyone.

I drifted into a sort of South Fork limbo: more a guest than a resident, less a child than a stepchild. I drove with Mom to drop off her bird-seed frogs at Whimsey's, a boutique general store in East Hampton. I spent weekends with Dad and Dolly in the home on Beach Lane, where Dad taught me to drive in Dolly's Audi, informing me I could control the accelerator better with my heel on the floor instead of in the air. One dreary week I earned money for college by cleaning the house's 1,400 window panes—every stinking one. I've hated washing windows ever since.

Sadly, my Wainscott haunts became haunted. By 1978 the Gehmans, Kaufmans and Nobles were all divorced families largely divorced from their East End neighborhoods. While Joyce Noble kept Whalebone Manor, her son Nick soon stopped spending entire summers in the Georgica Association, where we camped in that gnarly grove. The Kaufmans sold their rustic rancher on Whitney Lane, moved from their Manhattan apartment and bought a house in Chappaqua, N.Y., now owned by Bill and Hillary Rodham Clinton.

In the meantime my father became more of an authentic East Ender. He opposed strict zoning in letters to *The East Hampton Star*, sold his primitive paintings of Sag Harbor cottages built by whale-ship carpenters, shared a sermon on eternal life at the Bridgehampton Presbyterian Church. The Rev. Robert Battles, also the son of a minister, dipped into the Bible, reminding Dad that Christ asks the faithful to "leap for joy" even when they're hated. Dad dipped into his own bible, telling Battles there can be no hell worse than depression and no heaven better than when the black cloud lifts.

After Dolly sold the Beach Lane home, she and Dad moved into a small compound in Sag Harbor, a haven for the late John Steinbeck, one of my father's literary heroes. Dolly eventually tired of Dad's manic antics, which included flushing a perfectly good dinner down the toilet to punctuate an argument. In 1986 they divorced and Dad moved into the basement of the Sag Harbor Whaling Museum, then run by a pal of his. Soon he began shifting from rental to rental, infuriating landlord after landlord. In 1989 he settled in a seedy apartment above a store in Hampton Bays, about a mile from the railroad cottage where I began my South Fork life as a four-month-old. There he fulfilled a lifelong goal of starting a community newspaper. He reported, photographed, sold ads and rabbleroused.

Like Jake, Dad faltered without a female caretaker. Like Jake, he sabotaged himself with too much drink and too little Lithium.

In the summer of 1990 he was so unbearable that I left him early three straight times. The last time I was so desperate to escape, I began a four-hour drive at midnight. That fall Dad suffered a stroke shortly after I accepted he could never ditch his demons. In January 1991 Meg and I moved him to my apartment in Bethlehem, Pa., ending his days on the East End for good.

Over the next decade I was too busy to visit the South Fork. I wrote more than a thousand newspaper stories and two books. I moved my mother from New Rochelle to my two-family house in Pennsylvania. I moved my increasingly erratic father from an apartment to a residential-care facility to another residential-care facility to a VA clinic to a county home. Yet the South Fork kept caressing and clawing me, this time in a strange new way. I found myself arguing with writers for *The New York Times* and *New York* magazine who reduced the East End to a playpen for spoiled brats obsessed with getting the right raspberries, the right area code and permits to the right beaches. I couldn't stand that the Hamptons had become Hollywood East: glitzy, greedy, nasty.

Singer-songwriter Tom Paxton traces this great sea change to the time he was offered $30,000 for a red maple in his East Hampton yard. Someone was evidently hellbent on elevating their virgin property to an Insta-Estate. Paxton jokes that he and his wife were forced to move to Virginia because their class visa expired. "My car got too old," he says. "You can't get into a restaurant in East Hampton if you don't have a Lexus in the parking lot."

The biased, boring coverage compelled me to write a memoir restoring the South Fork's remarkable beauty and remarkable people. On July 22, 2001, 15 days after celebrity publicist

Lizzie Grubman created a media blitzkrieg by angrily reversing a Mercedes SUV from a fire lane and whacking 16 Southampton nightclubbers, *The New York Times Book Review* published my author's query, a miracle facilitated by the Hamptons hook. The next day I received e-mails from 11 former East Enders hungry to share the pleasant past. The next month I visited Wainscott for the first time in 10 years. Three months later Mike Raffel and I began tracing our old life among the dead.

# The Way of All Bone and Stone

The Penny Candy Shop in Water Mill closed in 2005, ending 44 years as the Peace Center of the Hamptons. *(Photo by Bill Hayward)*

I t's November 6, 2001, and Mike Raffel and I are waking the dead and the living in Wainscott Cemetery. Nearly two months after America's worst terrorist attack, and nearly a week after my family buried my father's ashes, we're memorializing our childhood.

We start by searching for Jake Murray's grave, so we can honor our honorary uncle. In the beautiful melancholy of late Indian summer twilight we weave between stones, calling out to Jake, trading tales about his terrible end. We remember his tortured third marriage, his botched suicide, his brief joy when *The New Yorker* published his short story about O'Phelan, an Irish-American writer viciously aware of his drunken insanity. Jake proceeded to fuck up a bright future at his favorite magazine by making himself a pest in its Manhattan offices, badgering Roger Angell, the very supportive fiction editor, for money and sanctuary. Jake's clothes were as ragged as his mind, which was jammed with CIA paranoia.

Jake's hope basically died on New Year's Eve 1976, normally a day for hopeful thinking, when a woman he was dating choked to death. Within the week he jumped into the East River, from a pier or a ferry. Four months later his body washed up off Staten Island. His corpse was so grotesque, he was cremated against his wishes. He was laid to rest on June 25, 1977, what would have been his 54th birthday.

Roger Angell, Jake's last editor, gave him a pair of fine farewells. In October 1977 *The New Yorker* published a second O'Phelan tale, left unfinished by Jake, with Angell fixing what he thought he would have fixed with the author. In April 2000, after accepting a distinguished-service award from the Authors Guild Foundation, Angell used his seesaw relationship with Jake to illustrate the frustrating, rewarding challenge of bringing out the best work of writers, especially when they're at their worst.

"These are good stories, first-class, and the best that Jake Murray could have done when he wrote them," said Angell, today a *New Yorker* senior editor and sports writer. "I have come to the conclusion that he understood this, and that he paid us at the magazine an amazing compliment by entrusting the rough second manuscript to us, when he saw that it was time at last for him to be moving along."

Even though the cemetery is only two acres, Mike and I struggle to find Jake's resting place. Our main problem is that we're distracted by old friends. We spend five minutes by the grave of a girl Mike dated. She was in her late 20s when she killed herself. She shares a plot with her sister, who also killed herself in her late 20s. The sad siblings remind us of four other Wainscotteers we know, or knew, who took their own lives. For a small cemetery, Wainscott has an awful lot of tragedies.

After 20 minutes Mike yells that he's found Jake's grave. The surprisingly small stone is the size of a large pitcher's rubber. The surprisingly bland inscription has only birth and death years and Jake's birth name, John F. Murray Jr. The universe is surely out of joint; surely, Jake should have left some smart-ass comment like "No Comment," the epitaph of fellow resident Richard Church, a Georgica Association member and an Arm & Hammer heir crippled in World War II. Church's snazzy signoff runs neck and neck with ex-trucker Leslie Shepherd's "I Told 'Em I Was Sick."

Still, the location of Jake's stone is perfect. Mike and I think it's wicked cool that our pal lies in line with one of the one-room school's basketball hoops, basketball being the game that fused us in front of Jake's studio-house on Foxcroft Lane. Better yet, the stone is near the center of the cemetery—the only time, in life or death, that Jake was near the center of anything.

The moment demands a Jake-like joke. I tell Mike what Howell Topping, the cemetery's longtime president and a sneaky comedian, told me about a new mansion shoehorned into a narrow lot by the cemetery's hedge. Hell, if the owner goes bankrupt, Topping figured, he can always turn the residential country-club clubhouse into a funeral parlor. Wouldn't the porte-cochere be perfect for parking hearses? And wouldn't the pool house with the chimney make a terrific crematorium?

Time has not been kind to my other South Fork sages. Norman Jaffe, my architectural hero, wrestled with his idealism and

Wainscott Cemetery is the final resting place of Jake Murray, the author's honorable uncle. *(Photo by Geoff Gehman)*

perfectionism while working with wealthy, cranky clients who demanded monuments to their monumental egos. In the 1980s he created a fair share of contemporary castles he dismissed as "pig-outs." He regained his vision and pride with Gates of the Grove (1987), a remarkable synagogue in East Hampton, and 565 Park Avenue (1993), an impressive office building in Manhattan. He nurtured his inner pedagogue by training his son as a designer, letting Miles turn his sketches on napkins and placemats into stairways, kitchens and most of an East Hampton house.

"Norman always lost money on architecture because he spent so much time and energy on making things right, on being incredible," says Miles. "Because you didn't think about the business, you thought about the design."

In the early nineties Jaffe was troubled by a difficult second marriage and the possible return of prostate cancer. On August 19, 1993, a month after changing his will, he piled his clothes neatly on a Bridgehampton beach, entered the ocean and disappeared. Two months later his pelvic bone washed ashore. Miles Jaffe knows in his heart that his father didn't drown accidentally, even though he was a terrible swimmer. ("Norman and water were like oil and water.") He believes that his father drowned intentionally, suicide being a logical choice for someone who thought he had run out of choices.

Today, Miles fortifies Norman's legacy from foundation to gable. His book *The Hamptons Dictionary* (The Disinformation Company, 2008) contains savagely satirical, Norman-esque entries about badly behaved invaders, including "Hummeroids" who park their military industrial-recreational complexes in "Garage Mahals" attached to "Angri-Las." The volume is dedicated to Norman, "who among other things, taught me how to make chicken salad out of chicken shit." Miles' renovation of and addition to his father's Leichter House (Bridgehampton, 1975) is Norman-esque in spirit: cozy, adventurous, sleekly organic. Miles is pleased by his first complete collaboration with a Norman building since Norman's death. The project projected him back to a happy period in the early eighties, when he and his father were knee deep in tracing paper, feverishly pursuing the art of architecture.

Jaffe's first South Fork landmark, the Becker House, closely resembles its original self, although it's a little less imposing behind a high hedge. The man who commissioned it, however, no longer lives there. "I sold it in the eighties before the enormous rise in property values on the South Fork—that's part of my peculiar genius," says Harold Becker, director of "Taps," "Malice" and other feature films. "Now I hear 'The Becker House' and that makes me feel even worse that I don't have it anymore. Of course it was unforgivable. I'll regret selling it to my dying day. But that's an abstract regret. The truth is, I lost heart in the whole area when all the nouveau riche came in with all those self-referential monstrosities that they put up to say: Hey, look at me. The locusts came and ate everything in sight."

Less than a mile from the Becker House, on Daniel's Lane in Sagaponack, my literary hero was consumed by other locusts. Truman Capote ruined friendships with assassin fiction. He ruined himself with booze, drugs and toxic revenge. He became a sad satire of the supremely confident writer who ended his 1968 *Playboy* interview—the interview Jake gave me as a gift—by boasting: "[I]f luck allows and discipline holds, I will have time to arrive at higher altitudes, where the air is thin but the view exhilarating."

Capote died in 1984, a bloated 59-year-old who could have passed for 79. Ten years later his ashes and those of Jack Dunphy, his longtime companion, were poured into Crooked Pond, part of a peaceful preserve between Bridgehampton and Sag Harbor. Like the couple's Sagaponack property, it's a retreat for birds—none as exotic, of course, as the spray-painted peacock born Truman Streckfus Persons. A bronze plaque on a boulder bears the sort of bounding, boundless sentence that made Capote my first favorite writer: "The brain may take advice, but not the heart, and love having no geography knows no boundaries."

Carl Yastrzemski, my baseball hero, never approached his 1967 heroics. Plagued by injuries, he had a long string of fair to middling seasons. Over his last 15 years he hit over .300 only twice and drove in over 100 runs only four times. He remained an exceptional left fielder, winning his seventh Gold Glove in 1977, and a clutch hitter, batting .310 in the 1975 World Series and driving in two of Boston's four runs during the epic one-game playoff against the Yankees in 1978. He also made the last outs of the '75 Series and the '78 tie breaker.

Yaz retired in 1983 as the first American Leaguer with at least 3,000 hits and 400 homers. He played his entire 23-year career with the Red Sox, a rare case of noble loyalty in an age of free-agent carpetbaggers. He remained heroically stoic, compensating for a painfully pulled Achilles heel by wearing a sneaker painted black to resemble a cleated shoe. Yet there was something grim about the ferocious way he clung to his baseball life, adjusting to his deteriorating body and skills by constantly changing his batting stance and equipment. Indeed, he confessed after his retirement that while he enjoyed the competition, he never had any fun. Playing the game, he admitted, was too much work and too little play.

Disappointed by Yaz's long decline, I skipped his 1989 induction into the Hall of Fame. Instead, my father and I held our own celebration, remembering the magical year he and Yaz became my battery mates. Dad didn't even mind when I told him I had lost the eight years of Yaz baseball cards I once pinned to the spokes of my Stingray.

Being a superstitious turncoat, I later used my Yaz legacy as a good-luck charm. In 2004 I rubbed his bronze plaque in the Hall of Fame before the Red Sox began a playoff against the Yankees. Result: the Sox became the first major-league baseball team to win a best-of-7 series after losing the first three games. After the final out I stood on the deck of my house and screamed "This one's for you, Yaz; this one's for you, Dad!" in the direction of my neighbor, a Yankee fanatic. In 2007, with the Sox down 3–1 to the Cleveland Indians in the playoffs, my mother served me three straight meals of ham on the plates she bought for our 1968 ham dinner with Yaz's parents. Result: the Sox won the next three games and advanced to the World Series, which they won for the second time in four years. Even after 40 years Yaz still had some major major-league mojo.

My racing hero, Mark Donohue, became a legend beyond the Bridgehampton Race Circuit. In 1972 he set a speed record while winning the Indianapolis 500. In 1974 he won the first International Race of Champions, a World Series for first-rate drivers, and released *The Unfair Advantage*, a unique memoir-manual. His advantage ended unfairly during a fatal crash while practicing

Richard B. Church, an Arm & Hammer heir crippled in World War II, left a bluntly humorous farewell on his stone in Wainscott Cemetery. *(Photo by Dennis D'Andrea)*

for the 1975 Austrian Grand Prix. He was preceded to the grave by another Bridgehampton favorite son, Peter Revson, who died while practicing for the 1974 South African Grand Prix.

By then the Bridge was running on fumes. The track was slowly strangled by anti-noise ordinances, poor access roads and lack of money to replace antiquated equipment—including wires hit by lightning after being exposed by eroding sand. In time it became a public course for club, motorcycle and Soap Box Derby racers, and a private course for cofounder Henry Austin Clark Jr. and other vintage-car gear heads. Cartoonist Charles Addams' third wife, Tee, knew her husband was coming home when she heard the roar of his 1926 Bugatti—a racket caused by a missing tailpipe or exhaust manifold—on the backroads between the Bridge and their house in Water Mill. "When she heard that raw engine screaming through the woods," says H. Kevin Miserocchi, executive director of the Tee and Charles Addams Foundation, "she would fill up the ice bucket and get out the cocktail glasses as though the commuter train were pulling into the station."

In 1983 a consortium of Bridge devotees saved it from becoming a condo complex. The Friends of Bridgehampton (now the Bridgehampton Racing Heritage Group) then helped new owner Robert Rubin, a Wall Street commodities trader and an owner-racer of classic cars, continue running it as a track until 1997. Rubin, the child of an appliance repairman, eventually transformed the property into an ultra-expensive Scottish-style golf course with a glass-cathedral clubhouse filled with contemporary art and racing memorabilia. The dunes that were hazards for drivers are now hazards for duffers. The Chevron pedestrian bridge remains as a strangely comforting relic, a reminder of the day I fell for fiberglass spaceships flying around blind hairpins.

Austie Clark's other grand South Fork venture, the Long Island Automotive Museum, had an inglorious end, too. In 1980 he closed the three-bay Quonset hut to the public after decades of decreasing revenues. He blamed his fall from grace on the Town of Southampton's refusal to let him advertise on billboards around town. He apparently didn't benefit enough from the extra traffic on the Montauk Highway after the 1972 opening of Exit 72 of the Long Island Expressway, which enabled motorists to bypass Riverhead and race faster to the East End.

In 1980 Clark auctioned many of his vintage vehicles in front of his museum. Being a natural ringleader, he naturally served as his own auctioneer. Dave Brownell, a fellow collector, appraiser and antique-auto historian, watched the sale with Charles Addams and another Clark crony. "We started making side bets about which cars would make the most money," says Brownell. "And Charlie Addams was really good. He won two-thirds of the bets. He cleaned our clocks."

Clark died in 1991, three years after Charlie Addams expired in one of his cars. By then the museum was a wreck; today, it's a dead mausoleum. The Quonset hut has a rusty façade, broken windows and skateboard graffiti. The gap-toothed sign reads "LONG ISLA MO IV M." The parking lot is a grove of rogue birch trees. It seems entirely fitting that nearby is a company that sells funeral monuments.

The museum is one of three ghosts from my childhood on the Montauk Highway. The Hamptons Drive-In in Bridgehampton died for good in the early eighties, killed by cable TV and the South Fork's first major shopping center. My movie passion pit was basically sacrificed for a W. T. Grant department store, a King Kullen supermarket and HBO's sexier stuff. Today, Victoria's Secret lingerie is sold near the site of the big screen where I watched Faye Dunaway and Steve McQueen play seductive chess in "The

Thomas Crown Affair." I remember that big screen whenever I have a soft-serve ice cream at the stubbornly antique Carvel across the highway, Bridgehampton's last drive-in.

The Penny Candy Shop in Water Mill, my sweetest pit stop, had a three-year demise. It began with the 2002 death of co-owner Harvey Morris and continued as his widow June recovered from a nearly fatal fall and electrocution in a doctor's office. She closed the store for good in 2005 on Christmas Eve, normally a great time for good will. She was assisted that day by Barbara Wilson, a Southampton judge who graduated with honors from June's candy charm school for young female merchants.

June fills her days baking, knitting under-helmet caps for overseas soldiers and raising money for charities. She can't believe that so many candy makers charge more for less. She still meets all sorts of folks who thank her for sweetening their lives. "I remember them more for what they bought than who they are," she says. "They'll introduce themselves and I'll look at them and say: 'Oh, you used to love the licorice buttons.'" She frequently visits Harvey's grave, which is in full view of their shop and the pole where he raised and lowered the American flag during rain, snow, sleet and cocktail party.

At least one of my Montauk Highway treasures is alive and lively. *The East Hampton Star* is still owned by the Rattray family, as it has been since 1935. It's still run by a mother publisher and her editor son, making it the rare American newspaper with two straight generations of parent-child bosses. It still publishes poetic photographs, well-lived obituaries and a town meeting of letters to the editor, a case study of democracy in black, white and gray.

In the seventies Jack Graves, my first journalism mentor, helped select, edit and stage seven decades' worth of *Star* letters.

"Five Writers in Search of an Editor" was performed at Guild Hall, located across Main Street from the paper's offices. "The idea being," says Graves, *The Star*'s sports editor since 1979, "that no matter how much time passes, more or less the same types appear on these pages. The crusading mother outraged by the decline of morals. The summer person eager to spread his wisdom amongst the hillbillies. The no-nonsense Bonacker who learned a thing or two about love on leave in France. The earnest booster afraid that if it gets out we have malaria here people might not come. And the writer of treacly verse, Lyrica Languish, who took exception to the fact it hadn't been mentioned she'd won fourth prize in Guild Hall's poetry contest."

*Star* letter writers and writers continue to chronicle the decline of East End beaches. In the 1960s and '70s owners of duneside homes tried to stall erosion with offensive jetties. Today, they're more likely to rebuild banks naturally, with sand worth more than $20 a square yard. Now, as then, nature laughs last. Every now and then a storm unearths bricks and radiators from the Georgian mansion buried in Wainscott in 1974 after the Town of East Hampton burned and razed it before it toppled onto Beach Lane beach. The debris surfaces by a house built on the unfortunate site, a Spanish villa that was nicknamed "Taco Bell" before Georgica Association leaders persuaded the owner to paint it less gaudy colors.

Now in its third century, the Georgica Association has managed to block most of the barbarians from its gate. With the exception of a hotel-fortress-bunker seemingly built for a South American dictator on the lam, the settlement remains gentle and genteel. Time passes slower and easier among the rambling brambles, the white-pebbled lanes that gleam like macadam beaches, the ship-shaped cottages slanted as if to send signals to one another.

Over the decades I've come to realize that Georgica is a lot like the rest of Wainscott: pristine and shaggy, exclusive and inclusive. In fact, the association's relationship with the community outside its gate rivals the relationship between Georgica Pond and the Atlantic Ocean, especially when the two waterways are connected by a channel bulldozed into the beach. That is, all the parties are independent, dependent, tidal. No matter what your status, you will damage the underside of your car if you speed over those speed bumps.

Outside the settlement's borders, the biggest changes involve two institutions most resistant to change. The one-room school is no longer the only school in town. In 2008 it was retired as a primary teaching center because it was too small, too inaccessible to the handicapped and too easily flooded. K-3 students now study next door in a much larger, much nicer building with two classrooms and two full-time teachers. The old school is used for Spanish lessons and recreational activities on rainy days. Its trash cans are used for trash, not for punishing trash-talking pupils.

Covered in weathered cedar-shake shingles, the newest Wainscott Common School looks like it's been around for 50 years instead of five years. Unfortunately, its erection basically eliminated the field where Mike Raffel and I played on the Wainscott Wildcats, trying to hit balls up the middle so they wouldn't end up foul in the cemetery. It's painful to see our old baseball rectangle surrounded by white PVC fence, masquerading as a horse paddock.

The general store, dead for a good 40 years, is no longer dead. The former home of fly paper festooned with dead insects and Mayflower-old carrots has been converted into a cheery garage for a snazzy hot rod owned by Dennis D'Andrea, a retired judge and Chauncey Osborn's grandson, and a snappy studio for Dennis' wife, printmaker Barbara Wilson D'Andrea, a retired art teacher who designed the cover of the Hall and Oates album "Abandoned Luncheonette." A hulk has become a hunk, making the view from Chauncey's grave much livelier.

Along the cemetery's northern border, beyond where the battered baseball backstop used to be, is a field owned by Pete Dankowski, my fellow former Wainscott Wildcat and the only full-time potato farmer who lives in Wainscott. He represents the last of six full-time potato-farming families active during the eight-decade lifetime of David Osborn, who belonged to one of the six. Yet, thanks to the land stewardship of David and his relations, Main Street remains as pleasantly pastoral as when I delivered the U.S. mail with Yaz, even though the one-room post office was long ago replaced by a bigger, duller building on the Montauk Highway. The meadow around Wainscott Pond, which is owned by David and his sister, remains a picturesque pasture of plenty, a sparkling spread for the cemetery's visitors and residents.

David still lives on Main Street, sharing a property with his son and his grandchildren, members of the 11th and 12th generations of Wainscott Osborns. In the summer he escapes the Hamptons crush to his house in Nova Scotia, which he bought in the 1980s in pursuit of a new refuge similar to his old one. He quickly learned you can never really replace your birthright retreat, that even a hurricane can't uproot six centuries of roots. "I went looking for another Wainscott," he says, "but found out it was here all along."

Sadly, my old Westwoods neighborhood feels like someone else's. On Whitney and Foxcroft lanes only the former Kaufman and Gehman homes are recognizable. I'm pissed that both houses have pools; in my day in the Westwoods, the only legitimate pool was the ocean. All the other buildings on Foxcroft and Whitney have been obliterated, either through renovation or demolition. Jake Murray's house-studio, for example, hides behind an eerily anonymous wall. "Man, Jake's probably rollin' now," says Mike Raffel. "He'd be seriously pissed that the city people took the country out of the country."

The strangest thing—stranger than the cottages replaced by mini-mansions, stranger than the ramshackle yards replaced by mini-estates—is the quiet. When Mike and I lived here, the Westwoods crawled with noisy kids, even in the off-seasons. The only people we met during our hour-long visit in November 2001 were a mother and child. She seemed unimpressed when we told her we're neighborhood alumni; her gaze was glazed. "Man, she didn't want to give us the time of day," said Mike as we drove away. "All the people in our time had time to give us the time of day. Hell, there's no one really here anymore. They just live here to vote."

Mike doesn't vote on the East End because he doesn't live there. Tired of rude people and poor schools, my carpenter pal sold the East Hampton house he built with materials salvaged from tear-downs. In 2003 he moved with his wife Carol and their four boys to Cambridge, N.Y., far from the crazy crowd. The village borders Vermont, a state where Mike happily vacationed as a kid. He digs the rural, relaxing vibe, which reminds him of the relaxing, rural vibe of our old Wainscott.

Mike frequently returns to the South Fork to work construction for his Uncle Denny, who trained him to be my rock 'n' roll guru. He stays in the East Hampton homes of his sisters Carol and Karen, the last Raffels left on the East End. "Wainscott" is part of Karen's e-mail address because Wainscott was, is and will always be her favorite address. As a youngster she secretly willed her parents to move there just so she could pick strawberries, which she can't do today because Wainscott no longer has a public strawberry patch.

I should be sad that all my childhood friends have left Wainscott. I should be mad that I couldn't afford to buy a house in my old home hamlet even if I sold 100,000 copies of this book. I should be, but I'm not. How can I be sad when a special place at a special time taught me how to be special? How can I be mad when the South Fork started the pilgrimage that made me the me I needed to be?

A naturalist. A movie buff. A jock. A rock 'n' roller. An architecture nut. A connoisseur of the feminine form. A lover of old social centers: general stores, penny candy shops, cemeteries, dead drive-ins. A journalist, a professional eavesdropper, a storytelling strategist of life's corkscrew turns. A middle-class dude with a classless attitude. A singer who can harmonize to anything—except that !@#%&? "Silver Bells."

My South Fork is a time-release capsule I can open wherever and whenever. I smell it in the perfume of privet blossoms. I taste it in a slice of coconut watermelon candy. I hear it in the hushed ocean roar of a stormy wind. I see it in Andrew Wyeth's painting "Her Room," which could be a portrait of the room where I almost lost my virginity.

And I feel it in this book, a castle between covers for the kingdom of the kid.

# NOTES AND (RE)SOURCES

Meg Gehman hams it up with the muggable Kaufman boys—from left, Whitley, Clayton and Douglas—on the Kaufman porch, May 1970. *(Photo courtesy of Clay Kaufman)*

## SPECIAL DELIVERIES

"For the death of the three-cent stamp": Thanks to Dennis D'Andrea for Sam Pierson's quip.

## THE WESTWOODS

Author interviews with Meg Gehman, Clay Kaufman, Doug Kaufman, Whitley Kaufman, Joe Raffel, Karen Raffel DeFronzo, Mike Raffel and Rosie Raffel.

## THE BEACH

Author interviews with Doug Benedict, Florence and Richard Fabricant and Tim Noble; information on battles over beach erosion and jetties from 1969–1971 articles in *The East Hampton Star* (thanks to Jack Graves for *Star* photocopies); information on Alfonso Ossorio and the Creeks from Steven Gaines, *Philistines at the Hedgerow: Passion and Property in the Hamptons* (Little Brown & Co., 1998).

"fogging up the windows": Thanks to Tim Noble for the quaint expression of lust.

Clay Kaufman had the surreal experience of picnicking at Napeague and seeing 30 grand pianos scattered around the giant dunes. On closer inspection he discovered they were just shells, props for a photo shoot for an album cover.

## THE SETTLEMENT

Author interviews with Doug Benedict, Bill Noble, Maggie Noble, Nick Noble, Tim Noble, Allan Montoya, David Osborn,

Norah Pierson, James Turner and George Walker; information on the history of the Georgica Association from G.W. Pierson's pamphlet "The Georgica Association, 1880–1948" (The Georgica Press, 1992), Donald Petrie's pamphlet "The Georgica Association, 1949–1992" (The Georgica Press, 1992) and association archives in the East Hampton Library's Long Island Collection.

"His tomatoes and the eggs from his chicken-house": July 6, 1968 minutes of Georgica Association board of directors, Georgica Association Archives, Long Island Collection, East Hampton Library.

"I'm Bobby Burns": Thanks to Denise Mannings for Pete Morrison's drunken rhyme.

## THE CEMETERY

I'm much indebted to David Osborn and Howell Topping for their tours of Wainscott Cemetery, where most of their relations are buried and where Howell was buried in 2004 under a headstone inscribed with a truck, a reference to his life as a farmer. "I promise to show you around," David told me before our visit, "as long as you promise to bring me home."

## THE DEAD STORE

Author interviews with Barbara Wilson D'Andrea, Dennis D'Andrea, Tim Noble, David Osborn, Norah Pierson and George Walker.

"salty, weather-beaten anecdotes": G.W. Pierson, "The Georgica Association, 1880–1948."

"Well, I don't know": The late Dayton Hedges, Wainscott's blind caretaker and all-around go-to good guy, quoted in *Our Hamptons Heritage*, Vol. 1, No. 2, Dan's Papers Ltd., 1984.

## THE SWEET SPOT

Author interviews with June Morris and Barbara Wilson.

## THE DRIVE-IN

Information on the Bridgehampton drive-in from newspaper clippings archived at the Bridgehampton Historical Society and 1967–1972 ads in *The East Hampton Star.*

## AUSTIE

Author interviews with Dave Brownell and Henry Austin "Hal" Clark III; information on Henry Austin Clark Jr. from Bridgehampton Race Circuit programs archived at the Bridgehampton Historical Society; information on some of Clark's vintage vehicles from Beverly Rae Kimes and Henry Austin Clark Jr., *Standard Catalog of American Cars, 1805–1942* (Krause Publications, 1996).

## THE BRIDGE

Author interviews with Mario Andretti, Guy Frost and Earl Gandel; information on the Bridgehampton Race Circuit from "Bridge" programs archived at the Bridgehampton Historical Society; information on Mark Donohue from Mark Donohue and Paul Van Valkenburgh, *The Unfair Advantage* (Bentley, 2000), and Michael Argetsinger, *Mark Donohue: Technical Excellence at Speed* (David Bull, 2009).

"This here is the end of the earth": David Pearson's comment about the Bridgehampton Race Circuit appears on www.

bridgehamptonraceway.com, the Web site of the Bridgehampton Racing Heritage Group.

"like a $10,000 bill must feel": Robert F. Jones, "Place in the Sun for Revvy," *Sports Illustrated*, January 10, 1972.

"the infernal machine": Paul Newman, foreword, Mario Andretti with Mark Vancil, *Andretti: Mario on Mario* (HarperCollins, 1994).

"just to make sure," "It just doesn't feel right": *The Unfair Advantage*.

"You know": Thanks to Earl Gandel for the Carl Jensen-Paul Newman anecdote.

## THE SPHINX

Author interviews with Harold Becker, Chico Hamilton and Miles Jaffe; information on Norman Jaffe and his architectural designs from Charles Langer, "Norman Jaffe in the Hamptons: New Architecture for a Traditional Resort," *Hamptons Magazine*, September 1980; Paul Goldberger, *Houses of the Hamptons* (Knopf, 1986); Alastair Gordon, *Weekend Utopia: Modern Living in the Hamptons* (Princeton Architectural Press, 2001), and Alastair Gordon, *Romantic Modernist: The Life and Work of Norman Jaffe Architect 1932–1993* (Monacelli, 2005).

## THE STAR

Author interviews with Florence Fabricant, Jack Graves, Laura Montant, Helen Rattray and Tom Paxton; information on *The East Hampton Star* from 1967–1972 articles, cartoons and photographs in *The Star*.

## MIKE & ME

Author interviews with Mike Raffel.

## YAZ, DAD & ME

Author interviews with Billy DePetris, the late Pete Michne and Tony Oliva; information on Carl Yastrzemski from Carl Yastrzemski with Al Hirshberg, *Yaz* (Viking, 1968), Carl Yastrzemski with Gerald Eskenazi, *Yaz: Baseball, the Wall, and Me* (Doubleday, 1990) and Carl Yastrzemski, *Yastrzemski* (Rugged Land, 2007); game-by-game accounts of the 1967 Boston Red Sox season from www.BaseballLibrary.com.

"Let me tell you something, pal": *The Boston Globe*, May 14, 2008.

## TRUMAN

Author interviews with Edward Albee, William Bayer, Robert Dash, A. E. Hotchner, Joe Petrocik and Myron Clement, Tinka Topping and Marina Van; information on Truman Capote and the South Fork from Rosemary Kent, "AD Visits: Truman Capote at Home in the Hamptons," *Architectural Digest* (January/February 1976); Gerald Clarke, *Capote: A Biography* (Simon and Schuster, 1988) and George Plimpton, *Truman Capote: In Which Various Friends, Enemies, Acquaintances, and Detractors Recall His Turbulent Career* (Nan A. Talese/Doubleday, 1997).

"like a drunkard's legs," "in a trance of greed": Truman Capote, *A Christmas Memory* (Random House, 1967).

"an exhilarating country lunch," "which I have forgotten," "*always* chilled": Anonymous [writing as Truman Capote], foreword, Myrna Davis, *The Potato Book* (William Morrow, 1973).

Another irresistible Capote caper comes from Dorothy "Tiger" Borland Kitt, my fellow former Wainscotteer. After locking himself out of his Sagaponack home, Truman visited the Wainscott house of Dayton Hedges, the blind caretaker for many South Fork residences. Capote rapped on Hedges' door and shouted for a replacement key in his notoriously squeaky, lip-smacking voice. "Who the hell," replied Hedges, "is that *woman?*"

## JAKE

Author interviews with Alison Gray, Dorothy "Tiger" Borland Kitt, Laura Montant, Jeff Murray, Melinda Murray McDougal, Karen Raffel DeFronzo, Mike Raffel, Rosie Raffel, Theron Raines and Patricia Wood.

"might swallow a baby": John Corry, *Golden Clan: The Murrays, McDonnells & the Irish American Aristocracy* (Houghton Mifflin, 1977).

"a wonderful sloshing trampoline," "as she had found," "From the shore": John F. Murray, *The Devil Walks on Water* (Bantam, 1970).

## SEX

Information on South Fork sexual politics from 1967–1972 articles in *The East Hampton Star*; information on *Playboy* from the magazine's 1967–1972 articles, interviews and pictorials.

# BOOZE

Author interviews with the Rev. Robert Battles, Pat Gehman, Erika Mark, Laura Montant, Jeff Murray, Mike Raffel and Rosie Raffel.

"double Russian vodka neat," "On eastern Long Island": John F. Murray, "O'Phelan's Daemonium," *The New Yorker*, May 24, 1976; thanks to Melinda Murray McDougal for the reprint.

# BARBERSHOP

Author interviews with Verne Behnke, Meg Gehman, Eunice Lopez and Bill Noble.

# THE TURNAROUND YEAR(S)

Author interviews with the Rev. Robert Battles, Meg Gehman, Pat Gehman, Tom Green, Susan Helier, Clay Kaufman, Doug Kaufman, Whitley Kaufman, Nick Noble, David Osborn, Tom Paxton and Mike Raffel.

# THE WAY OF ALL BONE AND STONE

Author interviews with Harold Becker, Dave Brownell, Barbara Wilson D'Andrea, Dennis D'Andrea, Earl Gandel, Jack Graves, Miles Jaffe, H. Kevin Miserocchi, June Morris, Tim Noble, David Osborn, Karen Raffel DeFronzo, Mike Raffel and the late Howell Topping.

"These are good stories": Roger Angell, "Remembering Jake Murray," speech for Authors Guild Foundation dinner, April 3, 2000.

"[I]f luck allows": Truman Capote, The Playboy Interview, *Playboy*, March 1968.

# THANKS, INC.

Pat Gehman, the author's mother, looking like a beach model in Wainscott, the hamlet between the Hamptons. *(Gehman Family Collection)*

It's hard writing about your life more than 40 years after it's been lived. It's harder writing about your life in a beach resort and farm community, where seasons blur like watercolors. It's even harder writing about your life in a beach resort and farm community scarred by alcoholism, divorce, suicide and other traumas you'd like to bury in the dirt or sand.

No wonder so many former Wainscotteers can't remember large chunks of their childhood. No wonder I thought seriously about putting a sandbox under my computer, so I could massage my memories along with my toes.

Fortunately, there were plenty of people who served as the sand under my feet. The following folks helped me build dunes of remembrance: Edward Albee, Mario Andretti, the Rev. Robert Battles, the late Mary Baxter, William Bayer, Harold Becker, Verne Behnke, Doug Benedict, Dave Brownell, Henry Austin "Hal" Clark III, Barbara Wilson D'Andrea and Dennis D'Andrea, Frances Mary D'Andrea, Pete Dankowski, Robert Dash, Billy DePetris, Florence and Richard Fabricant, Guy Frost, Earl Gandel, Jack Graves, Alison Gray, Tom Green, Chico Hamilton, Susan Helier, A. E. Hotchner, Lisa Michne Houston, Miles Jaffe, Doug Kaufman, Whitley Kaufman, Eunice Lopez, Denise Mannings, Erika Mark, the late John McCaffrey Sr., John McCaffrey Jr., Barbara Meyer, the late Pete Michne, H. Kevin Miserocchi, the late Laura Montant, Towny Montant, Allan Montoya, the late Carlos Montoya and the late Sally Montoya, Jeff Murray, Melinda Murray McDougal, Maggie Noble, Nick Noble, Tom Paxton, the late Norah Pierson, the late David Porter, Carol Raffel Fitzgerald, Joe and Rosie Raffel, Theron Raines, Helen Rattray, Charlotte Rogers, Peter Semler, the late Howell Topping, Tinka Topping,

James Turner, Marina Van, George Walker, Jared Wickware, Barbara Wilson, Patricia Wood.

Others who served the cause, knowingly or unknowingly: Roger Angell, Francis Barker, Judy Brennan, Paul Brennan, Gerald Clarke, Corinne Economaki, Steven Gaines, Alastair Gordon, Katherine Helmond, Peter Klebnikov, Howard Kroplick, Pete Lyons, Walter McCarthy, Tony Oliva, Joe Petrocik and Myron Clement, Ronald Radford, David Rattray, the late Leslie Wilson.

Thanks to these organizations: Bethlehem (Pa.) Area Public Library (especially Delia Paredes and Barb Subber), Bridgehampton Historical Society (especially Julie Greene), East Hampton Library, Group for the East End, *The New York Times Book Review*.

Thanks to photographers Theo Anderson, Bill Hayward and Chuck Zovko for their special skills and exceptional camera-raderie.

Thanks to James Peltz, co-director of SUNY Press, for his vision and enthusiasm, and to production editor Diane Ganeles, promotions manager Kate McDonnell and cover designer Amy Stirnkorb for their stellar stewardship.

Special thanks to *The Morning Call* in Allentown, Pa., for 25 rewarding years and the six months-to-life sabbatical.

This book is richer because of these kind kindred spirits:

Dorothy "Tiger" Borland Kitt, who recalled her late stepfather, Jake Murray, fondly and vividly.

June Morris, who with her late husband Harvey ran the Penny Candy Shop in Water Mill as a sanctuary of sweet citizenship.

David Osborn, who untangled Wainscott's tangled history and genealogy judiciously and humorously.

Clay Kaufman, who provided essential snapshots and indelible memories of the Wainscott friendship between his family and mine.

The late Jane "Ginger" Kaufman, who cared so well for my mother.

Bill Noble, who cared so well for my late father.

The late Tim Noble, who read every chapter carefully and gave me my first overnight stay in the Georgica Association in 40 years.

Karen Raffel DeFronzo, who offered marvelous accommodations, ceaseless support and the purest spirit of any fellow former Wainscotteer.

Mike Raffel, who after more than 40 years of friendship remains as wicked cool as Huck Finn.

My life is richer because of these steadfast friends: Gregg Cramer, Chuck Dervarics and Eileen O'Brien, Jodi Duckett, Gary and Pam Hassay, Jeff Matzkin, Helen McCole Bartusiak, Jack Murray, Bertie and Jim Musselman, June and Paul Schlueter.

R.I.P. Barba-Del Campbell.

Every memoir is an act of family therapy. One of the primary pleasures of writing this memoir was giving my mother Pat and my sister Meg a larger number of more pleasant memories of an often painful period. They have small roles on these pages but huge roles in my life.

*The Kingdom of the Kid* is lovingly dedicated to my father Clarence Harvey "Larry" Gehman (1923–2001), who settled us on the South Fork. Thanks to Dad, I befriended potato farmers and power brokers, chose Truman Capote and Carl Yastrzemski as role models, learned to throw a nasty curve and harmonize to "Silver Bells"—which I'm convinced is impossible to harmonize to, which makes it one of Dad's many booby traps. And, then, after six memorable years in Wainscott, he unsettled us, which started a four-decade pilgrimage that ended with this book.

After finishing the manuscript, I settled Dad's ashes around Wainscott, the happiest place of his frequently unhappy life. I sprinkled his cremains outside our old house on Whitney Lane; on the softball field and tennis courts in the Georgica Association; by the grave of Jake Murray, the surrogate brother he never really knew—or acknowledged. My final shrine was Beach Lane beach, where, predictably, the wind whipped the ashes into my face.

As I brushed my father from my eyes, it dawned on me that perhaps he was tricking me again, this time from the great beyond. Dad, after all, never really liked the ocean; he thought the beach was a bit of a bitch.

# ABOUT THE AUTHOR

The Gehmans—Pat, Meg and Geoff—in front of Austie Clark's Long Island Automotive Museum in Southampton, a candy store of vintage vehicles. *(Gehman Family Collection)*

Geoff Gehman is a former arts writer for *The Morning Call* in Allentown, Pa. He is the author of *Down But Not Quite Out in Hollow-weird*, an epistolary film biography of Eric Knight, a screenwriter for Frank Capra and author of the novel *Lassie Come-Home*. He lives in Pennsylvania's Northampton County and thinks about the long-lost Hamptons every day.

Geoff Gehman, Georgica Beach near Georgica Pond, June 2012 *(Photo by Bill Hayward)*

4801626R00148

Made in the USA
San Bernardino, CA
08 October 2013